That's
Not
English

That's Not English

Britishisms, Americanisms, and
What Our English Says About Us

— ERIN MOORE —

GOTHAM BOOKS

GOTHAM BOOKS

Published by the Penguin Group
Penguin Group (USA) LLC
375 Hudson Street
New York, New York 10014

USA | Canada | UK | Ireland | Australia | New Zealand | India | South Africa | China
penguin.com
A Penguin Random House Company

LIBRARY OF CONGRESS CATALOGING-IN-PUBLICATION DATA
Moore, Erin (Writer on English language), author.
That's not English : Britishisms, Americanisms, and what our English says about us /
Erin Moore.
pages ; cm
Includes bibliographical references.
ISBN 978-1-592-40885-6
1. English language—Variation. 2. English language—Spoken English—United States.
3. English language—Spoken English—Great Britain. 4. English language—Great
Britain—Usage. 5. English language—United States—Usage. 6. English language—
Usage. 7. Americanisms. 8. Great Britain—Civilization—Social aspects. 9. United
States—Civilization—Social aspects. I. Title.
PE1074.8.M66 2015
427—dc23
2014023302
Printed in the United States of America
1   3   5   7   9   10   8   6   4   2
Set in Harriet Text and Johnston ITC
Designed by Sabrina Bowers

Contents

Foreword

Reading Erin Moore's book, I suddenly realised a great truth. I was raised bilingual. Not that my Londoner parents took any pains in this department, but they were the first generation to have TV, and they considered it such a blessing to mankind that they never considered (for a single second) the option of switching it off. There were four things I absorbed about television from an early age:

1. You never switch it off.
2. American films are superior to British films.
3. Jumping up and down in front of the television to get parental attention is just childish and will be ignored.
4. American television is better than British television.

Thus I grew up watching *Bilko* and *My Three Sons* and *I Love Lucy* and *Dennis the Menace*. And I was happy. The dialogue wasn't so hard to understand, after all—once you knew that "candy" meant sweets, that "sidewalk" meant pavement, and that children said "Gee" at the start of every sentence. True, nothing in the sunny home lives of the Americans on television related to my own experience. We had no picket fence; we had no gigantic refrigerator; we had a markedly different climate. But theirs was self-evidently the pleasant reality, ours but the bathetic and murky shadow. No wonder I grew up believing that Americans were the only standard by which to measure one's own inadequacies. At the age of seven, I was reading a fairy story about a banished king and his daughter in which the king exclaimed, "Have we not blue blood in our veins?" and I went to my mum (who was watching television) and tugged her arm. "Mum," I said, "what colour blood have Americans got?"

This bilingualism was an illusion, of course. I did not speak American. The first time a waitress barked, "Links or patties?" at me in a real American diner, I was so confused that I wanted to cry. "I just want a sausage," I said lamely. Similarly, Erin Moore, before she came to live in England, believed she was a great Anglophile. Based in New York, she edited books written by British authors; she visited England frequently; she had British-born in-laws. However, nothing had prepared her for the day-to-day cultural chasms of misunderstanding that tiresomely divide the British English–speaker from the American. As this book so beautifully reveals, it's not just the vocabulary that is different: First, the vocabulary is symptomatic of much more; second, if you aren't pitch-perfect in your delivery, you still fail, and all your effort goes for nothing. Take the word "cheers."

The English say "chis" out of the sides of their mouths when

they mean "thank you" or "good-bye." Americans do not pick up
on this and instead say "cheers"—toothily, hitting the "r" a bit
hard and implying an exclamation point, whether they mean it
as a toast or as a casual good-bye. An English banker living in
New York groused, "I'm getting sick of my clients saying 'cheers'
to me. Americans say 'cheers' like Dick Van Dyke in *Mary
Poppins.*"

If you're a British person who has ever been confused by an
American saying that he "quite" liked you (apparently this
meant he liked you a lot, not that he was being mealy-mouthed),
or if you are an American constantly looking round for the phan-
tom gin and tonic that has elicited the bizarre British salute of
"Cheers!," this book will get to the heart of your alienation.
Word by troublesome word, Erin Moore delves into more cultural differences than you ever knew existed. A discussion of
"proper" takes us to the proper English breakfast (with links, of
course, not patties). This in turn leads to the latest item on the
Denny's breakfast menu: the Peanut Butter Cup Pancake Breakfast, which sounds like a heart attack on a plate but also would
probably be worth dying for. Similarly, the word "dude" takes us
on a brilliant digression concerning the bogus power of the British accent to intimidate Americans and also speculates on why
the British somehow can't bring themselves to adopt the term
"dude," no matter how much they happen to be exposed to it.

By the end of this book you will be impressed (as I was) that
the long-standing affection between our two cultures has managed to override all this mutual incomprehension for so long.
Why no international incidents caused by honest misunderstandings? Is it because we are both too polite to say when we
think there is a miscommunication? On a book-promotion tour

in America a few years ago, I was asked on live National Public Radio to talk about what Kingsley Amis had famously said about "berks and wankers" when it comes to preserving rules of grammar. "Now, Lynne, would you consider yourself a berk or a wanker?" asked the solemn broadcaster, with no apparent mischief in mind. Both words are, of course, rude in British English, but "wanker" is very rude indeed, a more potently offensive equivalent to "jerk-off," and you wouldn't expect a nice British lady to use it while discussing outmoded attitudes to, say, ending sentences with prepositions. But I was on live radio, and the chap had asked the question without embarrassment, so I just went along with it. I pressed on and explained what Amis had meant about berks and wankers, all the while praying that "wanker" was either meaningless in American English or meant something innocuous such as "clown."

As many of us know, straddling the Atlantic can be quite uncomfortable—and it doesn't help that the word "quite" doesn't always mean what you think it means. Being British, I can (infuriatingly) even have it both ways. I can say, "Are you quite sure?"—meaning "Are you positive?" But I can also say, shrugging, "Mmm, I'm only quite sure"—meaning I'm not sure at all. I can only apologise for the confusion that this linguistic imperiousness understandably engenders in others. No wonder the British are known abroad as slippery customers who never mean what we say and never say what we mean. We must appear like Humpty Dumpty in Lewis Carroll's *Through the Looking Glass*:

> "The question is," said Alice, "whether you can make words mean so many different things."

"The question is," said Humpty Dumpty, "which is to be master—that's all."

But I am so glad that such weaselly problems have led Erin Moore to write *That's Not English*. It is a brilliant guide to the revealing differences between two branches of English from a writer who is funny, smart, and almost worryingly observant. I was charmed from first to last. As an English person I will say, "Oh, jolly well done," but I'd like to add: "Good job!"

LYNNE TRUSS

Introduction

The idea that England and America are two countries separated by a common language is variously attributed to George Bernard Shaw and Oscar Wilde. Regardless of who said it, this ubiquitous line trivializes the problem. I've known Americans who made entire careers in the Middle East on a few lines of Arabic and conducted affairs in Paris without enough French to fill an éclair. So why do Americans, who arrive in England with an entire language in common, have such a hard time fitting in? And why do English people, who once set up homes in every far-flung outpost of their empire, find America so foreign?

What underlies the seemingly superficial differences between English and American English are deep and historic cultural divisions, not easily bridged. An American who moves to England is like Wile E. Coyote running over a cliff into thin air. It isn't a problem until he notices something is missing, and that something is the ground under his feet. An unscientific survey has shown that it takes about six months for an average expatriate to plummet into the ravine.

Eight years after moving to London from New York, I'm still having Wile E. Coyote moments. English people get a kick out of Americans cheering their children on at the playground because they would only say "Good job" with reference to a child's bowel movement. Americans are similarly bemused when the English shout "Well done!" because to them that's nothing but an unsophisticated way to order meat. Americans are wary of anything described as a "scheme" because in American English the word has nefarious connotations, whereas the English will talk about their "retirement schemes" or their "payment schemes" without guile. An American friend of mine got a huge unintentional laugh at her company's London office when she said, "I really have to get my fanny into the gym!" (If you don't know what's so funny about that, check *Mufti*, page 34.) You don't even have to stray into scatological or sexual realms to cause offense. Saying "couch" (or worse, "settee") instead of "sofa" is a class-baiting crime in some English households, but the only way to find this out is to trespass on the delicate sensibility. This particular social minefield does not exist for the American, who is allowed to bumble along in ignorance. But ignorance is not always bliss, as every expat learns.

The English abroad in America are less prone to such gaffes, since they have been exposed to American vocabulary and pronunciation through television, films, commercials, and other cultural exports for most of their lives. But landing in America can be overwhelming nonetheless. It isn't just that Americans make certain assumptions about the English character; it's also that having your own assumptions about Americans constantly confronted and challenged can be exhausting at first. We underestimate the culture shock involved when traveling between English-speaking countries at our peril. Once the novelty wears off, homesickness hits hard and fast. You can take nothing for granted.

England and the United States exist in mutual admiration and antagonism. This tension won't go away anytime soon, and it's regularly stoked. The BBC was inundated with suggestions after asking the public to submit their most reviled Americanisms. *The New York Times* reported Americans, in contrast, to be "Barmy over Britishisms." The differences in our language are most telling when it comes to vocabulary, which opens the door to a deeper exploration of how we think and who we are. The same word can have divergent, even opposite, meanings in England and America (*quite, proper, middle-class*). Some words exist in one English and not the other (*mufti, bespoke, dude*). There are words lionized by one country and reviled by the other (*whilst, awesome, shall*) and words that have connotations in one country that they lack in the other (*sorry, smart, ginger*). There are words that just sound *veddy, veddy* English, that Americans are more and more tempted to borrow willy-nilly, even when they don't always know what they are getting into (*bloody, shag, bugger, cheers, gobsmacked*).

These differences may charm, annoy, or obsess English speakers, but one thing is sure: They mark us wherever we go. And that is a good thing. Differences in language contribute to individual and cultural identity. They are interesting, valuable, and fun in themselves, but they are also the blazes on the trail. If you ignore or fail to understand them, you might as well be speaking a different language. You'll certainly feel lost in the wilderness. This book is a guide to English and American cultural differences, through the lens of language: the words we use that say the most about us, and why. It is a cultural history in miniature, and an expatriate's survival guide—from the United Kingdom, to the United States, and back again.

Joe Queenan once wrote that "Anglophilia, like pornography, is one of those things that are hard to describe but you know when you see them." I've always been one of *those* Americans. It runs in families. My nana gave me a pop-up book about the royal family and told me stories about her family's time in the Cotswolds while my grandfather enjoyed what had to be one of the cushiest postings of his air force career. At the age of five, I dragged my mother out of bed for a predawn viewing of Princess Diana's wedding. I still remember the nightdress I wore for the occasion. Mom was the one who woke me sixteen years later with the terrible news from Paris. For a certain cohort of American women, unlikely or silly or embarrassing as it may seem, these events were childhood's bookends. A hopeful and credulous part of us, awakened while watching Princess Diana's walk down the aisle, died a little during her funeral cortege.

Today, a new generation is delighting royal watchers worldwide, and giving souvenir makers a renewed revenue stream. The English have a lot to be proud of, having recently celebrated the marriage of the Duke and Duchess of Cambridge, the Olympics on home soil, the Queen's Diamond Jubilee, and the birth of a future king. American Anglophilia is at an all-time high, too. You know it when you see it.

It has been more than three decades since my sentimental education at Nana's knee. After studying nineteenth-century

British literature at colleges in America and England, marrying into an English/American family, and realizing the dream of becoming a dual citizen, let me tell you: Living in England really takes the edge off one's Anglophilia. What I loved before was not England itself, but the *idea* of England. Now my feelings, while still positive, are more complicated, attached as they are to specific people, experiences, and the circumstances of daily life in London with my husband, Tom, and our young children, Anne and Henry. As a sympathetic soul said to me during my first, rocky transitional year, moving to a new country is *jolly hard*! An American in England will always feel like a foreigner, and not always entirely admired—or welcome. Which is fair enough. American expatriates are a dime a dozen, particularly in London, and have been for a long time. In Hugh Walpole's *Portrait of a Man with Red Hair*, published in 1925, Harkness, an American expat on a train, is told by an Englishman, "If I had my way I'd make the Americans pay a tax, spoiling our country as they do."

"*I* am an American," says Harkness, faintly.

This may come as a surprise to Americans who have been to England on vacation, and spent a couple of madcap weeks seeking out everything they expected to find: legendary politeness and reserve, the much-vaunted stiff upper lip, Beefeaters, ravens, double-decker buses, infallible taxi drivers, Shakespeare, warm beer, pub lunches, and afternoon tea. Check, check, check, and check. Stereotypes confirmed, there is just enough time for a stop at Harrods before heading for Heathrow. Meanwhile, one of my English friends makes a compelling case that the English have more, culturally and temperamentally, in common with the Japanese than they do with Americans. That's why it is possible to spend months, and even years, as an outsider in the country and never penetrate beneath the surface to how people really live and think, and what their words actually mean. Though as time passes, one does begin to develop an inkling of just how much one doesn't know, and this actually helps. The similarities in our English can be misleading. It's the differences that give us direction and help us, finally, to know where we stand.

As late as the nineteenth century, it was feared that the two nations would lose their ability to communicate. Noah Webster predicted American English would one day be as different from the English spoken in England as Swedish and Dutch were from German. Thankfully, this never happened. What developed instead is a keen sibling rivalry. England plays the role of the cool older sister, trying to ignore the fact that pesky little America is now big enough to pin her to the wall.

Given their history, it should surprise no one that Americans were not always so enamored of Britishisms. In the early 1920s, H. L. Mencken sneered at English neologisms and the small class of "Anglomaniacs" who used them. He noted that the majority of Americans regarded everything English as affected, effeminate, and ridiculous. This, long before American moviegoers' obsession with Hugh Grant and Daniel Craig, though it was the theater that would later supply untraveled Anglophiles with "a steady supply of Briticisms, both in vocabulary and in pronunciation. . . . Thus an American of fashionable pretensions, say in Altoona, PA, or Athens, GA, learned how to shake hands, eat soup, greet his friends, enter a drawing-room and pronounce the words *path*, *secretary*, *melancholy*, and *necessarily* in a manner that was an imitation of some American actor's imitation of an English actor's imitation of what was done in Mayfair." If this seems an unnecessarily cruel assessment of the origins of Anglophilia, consider the source. Few partisans of American English have been as sure of themselves, or as committed to American individualism, as Mencken.

Believe it or not, there was once a time when British travelers could not praise American English enough. Relatively soon after America was founded, the English language spoken there sounded just archaic enough—free of the neologisms that corrupted that of their countrymen. But it wasn't long before America had neologisms of its own—such as *happify*, *consociate*, and *dunderment*—that sounded preposterous to English ears. America was too new and too young to pose a threat to their culture and language.

There is little love for an Americanism now. From the time of the first "talkies" (which were often translated for British audiences in the early days of the movie invasion), anxiety about American English's influence has spread. John Humphrys, venerable presenter of BBC Radio 4's *Today* program, admitted that as much as the English like to tell themselves (and, even more, the French) that their language has become the world's second language, they know that the lingua franca is actually American. Naturally, there is resentment that "our former colony has stolen our crown . . . The language is by rights 'ours,' so anything they might do to it is bound to be a debasement." It's no wonder that some people still think of the English spoken in England as the mother tongue, and the English spoken in America as its wayward child. But it isn't true. Today's English English, like American English, evolved as a dialect from sixteenth-century English, and neither can claim to be closer to the original.

What we are left with is the vanity of small differences, and we are more focused on them than ever. Greater access to travel and international journalism might be expected to cause a flattening-out of such differences in language, but ironically it has only increased our awareness of them. Cross-pollination is largely self-conscious, whether we embrace or avoid it. The American market routinely remakes English-language books and television for American audiences. Harry Potter's jumpers and biscuits become sweaters and cookies. *The Office* is remade with American actors (and their American teeth). Publishers and producers claim that they do this to make English exports more accessible. But many Americans resent it, and avidly ferret out the originals. Why would they, if they weren't seeking entrée to the preoccupations, idiosyncrasies, and oddities of the other culture? Not to mention shamelessly borrowing words to enhance their cultural cachet—call it *Masterpiece Theatre* syndrome. Shows that survive the move to America more or less intact—like *Downton Abbey*—do so because they are inextricable from their cultural setting and that is the reason Americans love them so much. (Just as the English love quintessentially American shows like *The Wire* and *Breaking Bad*.) When will publishers and Hollywood come to realize that the differences are valuable in themselves, and stop tampering with them? We should celebrate them instead, and by "celebrate," I don't mean "imitate."

In this book, I'll correct some popular misconceptions about both England and America and explain the subtleties that elude the cursory look, or the tourist on a ten-day tour. One of the most important of these is what it means to say *England* versus *Britain* or *the United Kingdom*. Great Britain includes the countries of England, Scotland, and Wales. The United Kingdom includes not just Great Britain, but also Northern Ireland. So only someone who is from England—the UK's largest country, containing 84 percent of its population—is English. Someone who is British might be Scottish, Welsh, Irish (from Northern Ireland), or English. Similarly, Americans, while resigned to being called Yankees by the English, have a narrower definition of the word, and it differs regionally. Southern Americans use *Yankee* to describe Northerners, and Northerners use it to describe New Englanders—the only Americans who identify *themselves* as Yankees (for more on this, see *Yankee*, page 179). England and America are diverse countries with a lot of different local accents and dialects, not to mention regional differences in vocabulary, which it would be impossible to do individual justice to. Still, to the extent that it is possible to generalize about them, I'll be doing just that. Anyone who would find out the truth has to start somewhere.

I pledge not to play favorites—as is only fair when speaking of siblings. My loyalties, like my language, are transatlantic. I refuse to choose sides—at least not permanently. I also refuse to relinquish my American accent, even if I adopt a few new words and allow my syntax to shift and adapt. Using English spellings still feels wrong, if not exactly treasonous. My father-in-law understands; he retains his English accent almost four decades after moving to America, yet his siblings tease him for what they feel is a thorough defection. A small (American) child once told my mother-in-law, "I'm sorry about Mr. Moore's disability," meaning his funny accent, a kind of speech impediment few people had in Tucson, Arizona, in the 1980s. I would say expatriates can't win, but it isn't really true. I think we have the best of both worlds.

As a former book editor who specialized in finding and publishing British books for American readers, I know how fruitful cultural tensions can be. I am a passionate and curious reader and observer of the way people talk, and the ways we understand—or misunderstand—one another. This subject is a moving target, and extremely subjective. You are bound to disagree with me at times. My hope is that this book will help Americans and the English communicate better, or at least understand why we don't.

That's Not English is for you if you love language enough to argue about it; if you enjoy travel, armchair or otherwise; if you are contemplating a move to England or America; if you consider yourself an Anglophile; or if you've ever wondered why there isn't a similarly great word for English people who love America. (*Americanophile* feels like a mouthful of nails, and *Yankophile* sounds truly disreputable.) This is a love letter to two countries that owe each other more than they would like to admit. God bless us, every one.

Quite

In which we find out why Americans really like quite
and the English only quite like really.

What harm could an innocent little adverbial modifier do? Look no further for evidence than *quite*, which has been the cause of confusion, unemployment, heartbreak, and hurt feelings, all because of a subtle—yet vital—distinction that is lost on Americans, to the consternation of the English.

Both nations use *quite* to mean "completely" or "totally." This meaning dates to around 1300, and applies when there is no question of degree. If you say a person is "quite nude" or a bottle is "quite empty," it might sound oddly formal to the American ear, but it will cause no controversy or misunderstanding. Nude is nude. Empty is empty. The trouble begins when *quite* is used to modify an adjective that is gradable, like "attractive," "intelligent," or "friendly." For, then, the English use *quite* as a qualifier, whereas Americans press it into service as an emphasizer. In English English, *quite* means "rather" or "fairly," and is a subtle way of damning with faint praise. To an American, *quite* simply means "very," and amps the adjective. No subtlety there.

Is anyone surprised? The stereotypes of the discerning Brit and the hyperbolic American have as much currency now as they ever did. American adjectives have always gone up to eleven. English visitors to a young America were amazed by the tall language they heard—words like *rapscallionly*, *conbobberation*, and *helliferocious*. Such words seem outlandish today only because of their unfamiliarity. Whether or not they were widely used in the Wild West, they made Americans seem badass. Everyone, not least the milquetoasts back east, wanted to believe in an America that was unleashed and not quite housebroken.

These words beggar *awesome*, a widely derided modern example of American hyperbole. Once, only God could be awesome. Now even a mediocre burrito qualifies. It wouldn't be so bad if *awesome* hadn't been aggressively exported. A post on urbandictionary.com rings with contempt, describing *awesome* as "a 'sticking plaster' word used by Americans to cover over the huge gaps in their vocabulary." Here, *sticking plaster* is the dead giveaway to the poster's nationality.

Another Englishman who has come out, bravely and publicly, against *awesome* is a poet who works in a Los Angeles bookstore (imagine!). John Tottenham's campaign to stamp out the word *awesome* (which he told the *Daily Mail* was "bogus") extends to an "Anti-Awesome oration" and some snazzy bumper stickers. He devoted an almost American level of enthusiasm to the task before pulling himself up short at having T-shirts made, which would have been taking it too far. He was the one who chose to live in LA, after all. You can't very well move to the beach and complain about the sand.

American enthusiasm was once an object of admiration. An English novelist named Mrs. Henry De La Pasture was quoted in *The New York Times* in 1910: "The Americans have been obliged to invent a new verb for which we have no use over here—'to enthuse.' Why don't we enthuse? And why, if we do conjugate this verb in secret, are we so afraid to let it be known? . . . We fear terribly to encourage ourselves or others. The people over there are not afraid. They let themselves go individually and independently over what they like or admire, and pour forth torrents of generous praise which we should shrink from voicing unless we were quite sure that everybody else agreed with us, or unless the object of our admiration had been a long time dead." The English may detect a note of condescension here, but an American won't.

Americans overdo, overstate, overenthuse—it has ever been and ever will be. So it's tempting to make fun of Americans for press-ganging *quite*, an unassuming qualifier, to their own eager ends. But you'd be wrong. When *quite* modifies a gradable adjective, the UK usage—not the American—is the deviation. The American use of *quite* to mean "very" began around 1730, whereas the English sense of *quite* as a qualifier wasn't recorded until more than one hundred years later, in 1845. And it has been causing international incidents ever since.

An English author receives an editorial letter from her American editor who "quite" likes her new book. (Insult!)

An American student finds it impossible to get a job in the UK based on the glowing recommendation letters submitted by her professors, whose highest praise is "quite intelligent and hard-working." (Shock!)

An English houseguest confesses to being "quite hungry" and is served a steak of punishing size by an oblivious American friend. (Horror!) And so it goes.

It doesn't really matter who started it—the root of this misunderstanding over *quite* is a difference in the way Americans and the English habitually express themselves. As anthropologist Kate Fox explains in her fascinating book *Watching the English*, "our strict prohibitions on earnestness, gushing, emoting and boasting require almost constant use of understatement. Rather than risk exhibiting any hint of forbidden solemnity, unseemly emotion or excessive zeal," the English feign indifference. "The understatement rule means that a debilitating and painful chronic illness must be described as 'a bit of a nuisance'; . . . a sight of breathtaking beauty is 'quite pretty'; an outstanding performance or achievement is 'not bad'; . . . and an unforgivably stupid misjudgment is 'not very clever.'" Anything that would warrant streams of superlatives in another culture is pretty much covered by "nice."

What is an American interlocutor to do? Look no further for advice than Debrett's, the self-proclaimed "trusted source on British social skills, etiquette and style . . . originally founded as the expert on British aristocracy." Debrett's warns against mistaking understatement for underreaction: "read between the lines and you'll find the missing drama and emotion."

But how can Americans, renowned for their obtuseness, be expected to read between the lines when the English consider "Quite" a complete sentence? Would it be easier if the English learned to take the American *quite* with a grain of Maldon salt? Quite.

Middle Class

In which we find a far more stable class hierarchy in England, where class and cash are but loosely linked.

Catherine Middleton, Duchess of Cambridge, is so happily ensconced in the heart of England's royal family now, so beloved by practically everyone, it would be possible to forget the tabloid nastiness that erupted after her 2007 breakup with Prince William. It was said that the prince broke it off, in part, because of Ms. Middleton's background—in particular, her mother's overly obvious glee at the potential match, and Mrs. Middleton's subroyal behavior, which allegedly included chewing gum and using the word *toilet* (see *Toilet*, page 55). Snobs reveled in the knowledge that Mrs. Middleton had once worked as a flight attendant, and friends of William's were said to have intoned "Doors to manual" in Kate's presence. To his credit, the prince and his aides dismissed these rumors in the strongest terms. But the English media are notoriously prone to public shaming, and the way they interpreted the breakup surely says more about the English fascination with class than it does about Catherine or her solidly middle-class family, in particular her mother, who always appears impeccable.

Class warfare supposedly died out years ago in England. Back in 1997, former Labour MP John Prescott (now Lord Prescott) famously declared, "We're all middle class now." But don't you believe it. As cultural commentator Peter York has said, although "everywhere has a class system . . . it's our obsession in the sense that race is the American obsession."

Productivity plummeted in April 2013 when the BBC's class calculator began making the rounds of social networking sites. The calculator was part of a larger project, the Great British Class Survey. A brainchild of BBC Lab UK, it aimed to find out whether the traditional hierarchy of "working," "middle," and "upper" classes still existed and whether or not social class "even matters" in twenty-first-century Britain. They got their answer when five million people logged on to find out where they stood and proceeded to argue over the methodology that had divided the nation into seven distinct classes with new names: Elite, Established Middle Class, Technical Middle Class, New Affluent Workers, Traditional Working Class, Emergent Service Workers, and the "Precariat," the "poorest, most deprived class."

The class calculator released to the public (although apparently derived from research conducted privately with much longer questionnaires) based its scores on only five questions. The first three were measures of cold, hard cash: income, renting vs. owning a home (and of what value), and amount of savings. The final two questions in the class calculator—preferred leisure activities and the variety of professions within one's social circle—were not weighted heavily enough to counteract the influence of the crass cash-flow questions. This was controversial because the English consider how *much* money one has a weak indicator of class—how it was acquired and what one chooses to do with it matter far more. I experimented by giving identical answers for the "friends" and "culture" questions, varying only my answers to the financial questions, and was assessed at nearly opposite ends of the spectrum: first "Elite" and then "Emergent Service Worker." So it's easy to see why the class calculator was considered a blunt instrument by many.

A majority of both Americans and English people describe themselves as middle-class. However, as we have seen, just because they use the same words doesn't mean that Americans and the English are thinking the same way. In America, the middle class is more an economic category than a state of mind, and membership in it is not predicated on as many complicated and specific class markers. Where Americans shop, what they buy, and how they entertain themselves are only mild predictors of whether they will identify as middle-class. The same is not true in England, where membership in the middle class is more dependent upon being the product of specific types of families and schools, and the shared tastes that one develops as a result.

The artist Grayson Perry, in his documentary *All in the Best Possible Taste*, divided the English middle class into two tribes with different preoccupations. Both tribes are defined by their consumption, but whereas one is more about shopping and identifying with known brands (clothing, cars), the other defines itself by education and ideas, primarily consuming culture (performances, exhibits). Members of both tribes share a similar anxiety about appearances and the desire, above all, to be appropriate and "get it right." In short, both branches of the middle class care deeply what others think and are liable to try too hard—and to disagree strenuously about what signifiers mark the middle.

In my experience these tribes are far from distinct. Both culture and commerce have a place in the middle-class heart, as do peremptory judgments about how others might choose to spend their time and money. But American and English attitudes toward the middle class are very different. In brief, the English middle class likes to make fun of itself, and comes in for a lot of mocking, both good-natured and otherwise, from other classes. In England, making fun of the middles is a national sport. Americans are far more serious—and sentimental—about their middle class. Why? It all comes down to social mobility and self-consciousness.

There is less social mobility in England, so the middle class is more stable and secure from generation to generation. It is seen by outsiders as quite privileged—and possibly more than a little bit smug. Because of this, its members are far less worried about losing their place in society than they are about drawing the enmity of other classes. The middle needs approval to enjoy the spoils of its position (Barbour jackets, cottages in the country, organic produce boxes, fancy cheeses, Range Rovers—aka Chelsea tractors—Farrow & Ball's twenty shades of white paint, and the like), so they mustn't ruin it for themselves by boasting or appearing to strive, but instead make themselves as charming and likable as possible. In England, this is achieved through self-deprecation—jokes at one's own expense. Sharp-eyed observers have noted that at one extreme, this self-deprecation can become boastful, as it shows one is so comfortable, so confident, that one can choose to appear less so. The delicate art of the humble-brag was made for the English middle class.

In England, mocking the middle is a way to distance yourself from it while still enjoying its comforts. Friends of mine who are indisputably among the elite in England, whether by virtue of hard work, birth, or both, are fond of doing down (disparaging) the middle class as if from a lower point on the socioeconomic ladder. It takes on a pejorative ring. "That's so middle-class," they'll snort—meaning boring, bourgeois, predictable, uncool. As one man wrote before taking the BBC class quiz: "If I'm middle class, I'll fill a 4 x 4 with organic pesto and drown myself." The English can afford to be lighthearted about their middle class, knowing all the while they form the backbone of the country, providing political and economic stability. As David Boyle pointed out in *The Guardian*, "Without the middle classes there is no hope for the poor either . . . The alternative to a thriving middle class is a new tyranny by the few who own everything." As an American reading this, I felt a queasy sense of recognition. Many Americans fear that this is exactly the direction the US economy is taking, and their fears seem justified.

In America, where there is no proscription against hustle, and birth to a certain kind of family is no guarantee, people aspire very earnestly to join the middle class, and those on the inside actively fear falling out. This is a real possibility. According to a recent survey by Pew, the number of Americans self-identifying as lower-class or lower-middle-class increased by 25 percent between 2008 and 2012. The greatest increase was among the young. Americans between the ages of eighteen and twenty-nine, having come of age in a recession, were far more likely to place themselves in the lower brackets. Three-quarters of Americans said that it was harder to advance than it had been a decade ago, and parents no longer believed that their children would grow up to live better than they did.

These anxieties are central to life in America now. The middle class is the country's largest political interest group, and politicians both liberal and conservative constantly appeal to it, defining it even more broadly than demographers would—beyond a mere income category. The term *middle class* has become symbolic of aspiration itself. During the last presidential election, in a campaign stop in Parma, Ohio, President Obama made it clear that his personal definition included the poor: "I want to say . . . that when I talk about the middle class, I'm also talking about poor folks that are doing the right thing and trying to get to the middle class. The middle class is also an attitude. It's not just about income, it's about knowing what's important . . . your values and being responsible and looking after each other and giving back." It is essential that an American politician appear as middle-class as possible, and bring as many voters into that circle as he or she can, because belonging to the middle class is the *right thing* to aspire to.

In England, politicians have a difficult balancing act. They, too, must appeal to the middle-class majority, but they must do it while trying not to appear too middle-class themselves. They would risk alienating not only working-class voters, but also many in the middle who roll their eyes at inherited privilege even as they enjoy it themselves. Because in England, membership in the Establishment carries not only positive connotations, like working hard, wanting the best for one's children, and stretching culturally, but also uneasy ones, like the possibility of the better-off conspiring against the worse. Lawrence James, in *The Middle Class: A History*, gives evidence that audible trappings of status have lapsed. Politicians who have been to private school and "Oxbridge" (Oxford or Cambridge universities) typically hide their posh accents to avoid charges of condescension because "in public life it is now a handicap to sound even remotely like Bertie Wooster." The last fifty years have seen the rise of not only Margaret Thatcher, who never let anyone forget she was a greengrocer's daughter, but Ted "Grocer" Heath and John Major—the first prime minister not to have attended college (or, as the English say, "gone to university"). In fact, David Cameron is the first Tory *toff* (member of the upper class) England has elected prime minister in a generation.

In England, because class is so much more than an income category, it usually takes more than one generation for a family to achieve true class mobility. A family might earn enough to place them in the middle, but lingering working-class accents and tastes can be a sign that their roots—and refusal to put on airs that would be seen through anyway—are a source of pride. The desire of members of the English middle class to appear less posh has even given rise to "mockney"—a fake Cockney accent used by middles to downplay their origins and borrow some working-class cred. Tom Heyden, a twenty-five-year-old university graduate from a London suburb, writing in response to the class calculator, admitted most of his school friends did this. "I went to a private school. It wasn't the type of school with *Downton Abbey* accents. Many of the kids talked more like the crack

dealers from gritty dramas." You aren't supposed to believe
these put-on accents, but you are supposed to buy into the de
facto rejection of certain *naff* (silly) attributes of the middle
class, like caring about accents.

I think it's safe to say that Americans on a similar class jour-
ney take on the trappings of the middle class as soon as possible,
and with fewer negative social consequences. It helps that these
days, although regional distinctions persist in American accents, class distinctions have largely disappeared. (No one in
New York today speaks like Franklin Delano Roosevelt, the
quintessential New York aristocrat of the early twentieth century.) The middle class in America has historically taken its role
as the backbone of the country and the keeper of its ideals very
seriously. Yet the middle is shrinking. The fluidity of social mobility in the United States is like a roller coaster—exhilarating
when you're up, and nauseating when you're down. But the reason the middle class is beloved—not mocked—by those within
and without, is that hope springs eternal. If you're down today,
you could be up tomorrow. As James Fallows wrote in the *National Journal*, "Because I'm middle class, I have something in
common with my neighbors and fellow citizens. The United
States has been at its best politically and economically when we
have viewed other members of society as 'us' rather than
'them.' "

This explains why Americans have always loved Kate Middleton so much, while England was busy resisting her charms
until the moment it became clear she was the chosen one. Americans can't imagine why anyone wouldn't want a middle-class
commoner—one of *us* rather than one of *them*—for a queen. Interestingly, though, many English women of similar age and

class to the Duchess of Cambridge would admit to having, at least once, imagined filling her shoes. "It could have been any one of us," said an English friend, sounding, for one unguarded moment, like a little girl in a princess dress—or an American. Kate had America at "hello" because, let's face it: It's hard to think of a more stylish way to fall out of the middle class.

Moreish

In which we are surprised to discover that the English eat
more chocolate than Americans do.

Of all the words Americans have borrowed from the English, words with little cultural congruence, words that make them sound pretentious, or silly, or both (see *Cheers*, page 59), it is surprising the words that have been missed. Words that chime with the American character and would seem right at home. Words that would not make an American sound as if he or she had just returned from a junior year abroad. One such word is *moreish*, an adjective describing the quality of certain foods that makes one want to keep eating them. But you wouldn't say, "That *sous vide* pigeon with morel reduction is really moreish," even if you thought so. Because this word is really more about movie popcorn, salted peanuts, chocolate-covered raisins, malted milk balls . . . No

word implies the hand in the snack packet quite like *moreish*. So why don't Americans have this word? No one outsnacks an American. Or so I thought, before moving to England.

The English are great snafflers. To snaffle is to eat something quickly, and sometimes without permission. Snaffling is what you do with the last brownie in the breakroom, or the chocolate-covered biscuits that you bought "for the children." Snaffling is to the kitchen cabinet what foraging is to the wilderness.

If the English snaffle, Americans prefer to mainline their snacks, typically on the run. Unlike the English, Americans do not have much allegiance to set mealtimes. Restaurants serve nonstop. Carryout and to-go containers are masterpieces of engineering. Think mini Oreos that you can pour into your piehole from a twelve-ounce cup. Think "big grab" bags of Cool Ranch Doritos. Or a "go sack" of Smartfood. (Translation for non-Americans: This is a magically delicious cheese-flavored popcorn.) Think chips made in the shape of little shovels, so as to hold a maximum quantity of dip. The equivalent large packages in England will say, in a large, admonishing font, "great for sharing!" or "love-to-share pack." American snacks may be labeled "family-size" but, conveniently, the size of the family is not specified.

Ironically, it was American snack companies that also pioneered the practice of charging more for far *less* food, in the form of "100-calorie packs" containing five Cheez-Its or half a dozen creamless Oreo wafers, and if there's anything more depressing in Snackdom, I don't want to know. In America there is no middle way. You're strapping on the feedbag, surrendering to

your animal urges, or paying the Nabisco police to help you com-
bat them. Americans like their snacks to come with health
claims: low-fat, gluten-free, no trans fats, calcium-enriched,
multigrain. They like it so much that one of the most effective
diet tips ever marketed in the United States was Michael Pol-
lan's "avoid food products that make health claims."

The English aren't as into health claims as they are the concept of luxury—a word not generally associated with foodstuffs
in America. Anything from a bag of granola to a box of choco-
lates can be labeled as *luxury*, almost as if to reassure a wary
public. If it says *luxury*, it must be posh nosh. When you consider that, in living memory, potato chips, or *crisps*, came with
a little packet of salt that you had to add yourself, maybe it is not
so surprising. The flavoring technology simply didn't exist. This
is why bags of crisps are often labeled "ready salted" in England,
even now. It's as if the manufacturers are saying, "Don't take
these presalted crisps for granted, people."

Perhaps such privation is what paved the way for the absolute
riot of taste combinations that awaits English crisp snafflers
today: hog roast, beef and Yorkshire pudding, pickled onion,
prawn cocktail, sweet chili, smoky bacon, lamb curry, Worces-
tershire sauce, and sausage and ketchup flavo(u)rs, just for a
start. Americans—who normally view variety as a birthright—
nevertheless find this a bit nauseating. They do love their barbe-
cue and sour cream and onion—heck, even a little salt and
vinegar from time to time, to mix things up. But beef and lamb
flavor? No, thanks. Ask many expat Americans what snack they
miss most and they will say Pirate's Booty, little puffs made from
cornmeal and rice, flavored with "aged white cheddar," and

"baked perfectly to pirate standards." Clearly the English do not know what they are missing and have few pirate standards to speak of.

So you can see that while America and England are both snack-centric cultures, they do not always agree on what is moreish. For example, Americans might be surprised by the variation in social norms about when and how much peanut butter is appropriate to eat. Many Americans consider peanut butter a perfectly reasonable breakfast food, and why not? It probably has as much protein as eggs, and it goes better with syrup. The English don't necessarily object to peanut butter, but they ingest it in far smaller quantities. The largest jar of peanut butter you could find in an English supermarket would fit cozily inside a child's shoe. The largest one you would find in America is a gallon-size bucket with a handle, the better to swing it into the back of your minivan. The English generally do not touch peanut butter before noon, but many of them like their toast with Marmite—a sticky brown paste made of yeast extract. Which is grosser? I think we can answer that objectively.

No one believes me when I say it, but the English have a much sweeter sweet tooth than Americans. The cookie, or biscuit, offerings in an English supermarket are as varied as they are in America, but more of them are marketed to adults. Sweets (or sweeties)—nonchocolate candies—are a lifelong indulgence and, for some, an obsession. Strong flavors are more common than they are in America. (An exception to the rule is Altoids, "The Original Celebrated Curiously Strong Mints," which originated in eighteenth-century England, and whose nostalgic tins are now made in Chattanooga, Tennessee.) English lemon-and-pear drops (described by Roald Dahl in his memoir, *Boy*, as "smelling of nail varnish") could burn the enamel off your teeth. Bendicks Bittermints are Peppermint Patties to a power of ten—in a distinctive dark green–and-gold box that proudly proclaims Bendicks' Royal Warrant, "By Appointment to Her Majesty the Queen." Liquorice Allsorts look like little pastel plastic Lego bricks but taste, to the American palate, like purest evil. Aniseed balls are dusky purple and, as advertised, taste like aniseed—another candy it is hard to imagine children going for, but English children do. In America, by contrast, Sour Patch Kids (sweet gummies coated with sour sugar) and Pop Rocks (tiny candies that are carbonated, creating tiny explosions in the mouth) are considered daring, and M&M's are the bestselling candy.

This is not to say that the English don't love chocolate, too. They put away about ten kilos per person, per year—roughly twice as much as the average American—and their bestselling bar is Cadbury Dairy Milk. But on the subject of American chocolate, they are united in disgust. The masters of understatement have proclaimed Hershey's to taste of "cat vomit," "poo," and "sour milk." It is widely known to English expats that even Cadbury-branded chocolate is not safe in America because, as one bitter chocolate-lover put it, "Cadbury made the mistake of letting the disgusting Hershey company of weasels fool around with the recipes . . . in America as part of a marketing and distributing scheme." It is true that the manufacturing methods are different. A Cadbury Dairy Milk bar contains 23 percent cocoa solids, whereas a Hershey bar contains just 11 percent. The first ingredient in the Dairy Milk is milk; in a Hershey bar, it's sugar. And, as Julia Moskin reported in *The New York Times*, although Hershey's process is a closely guarded secret, "experts

speculate that Hershey's puts its milk through controlled lipoly-
sis," causing the fatty acids in the milk to break down. This pro-
duces "butyric acid, also found in Parmesan cheese and the
spit-up of babies . . . a distinctive tang that Americans . . . now
expect in chocolate." To each his own.

For most people, the preference for one brand or snack over
another comes down to childhood tastes and the memories associated with them. The English may never become converts to
Hershey's chocolate, and Americans may never embrace Marmite. But Americans might want to make a habit of *moreish*. I
promise not to make fun of anyone borrowing this Britishism—
as long as you save some M&M's for me.

Mufti

*In which we find out why the English
love uniforms so much.*

Mama, that girl has a red cardigan! And that one, and that one . . ." I explain why most of the children in our neighborhood always seem to be wearing the same outfit: It is their school uniform. My three-year-old looks quizzical. "But what's 'uniform'?" As we keep walking toward Edgware Road—past the children in their red jackets and cardigans; past the policemen in their helmets and the street cleaners in yellow reflective vests; past the grocery store where the workers all wear green smocks; past the *shisha* cafés where women in hijab sit drinking tea—I realize that almost everyone is wearing a uniform. Around here, you need a word to describe the state of *not* being in uniform. And the English have one: *mufti*.

Mufti has been the slang term for plain clothes in the British Army for more than two hundred years. Army officers, in their downtime, often wore dressing gowns, smoking caps, and slippers that resembled the traditional dress of a Muslim cleric. A mufti is an expert in Islamic law who is entitled to rule on religious matters, for example issuing a fatwa. This is an odd juxtaposition, to say the least, but *mufti* is just one of many words the English borrowed from India. A comprehensive list can be found in Henry Yule and A. C. Burnell's *Hobson-Jobson: Being a Glossary of Anglo-Indian Colloquial Words and Phrases and of Kindred Terms, Etymological, Historical, Geographical and Discursive* (1886). Other *Hobson-Jobson* words include *khaki*, *pyjamas*, *veranda*, *loot*, *pukka* (genuine), *shampoo*, *doolally* (crazy), and *jungle*.

Many *Hobson-Jobson* words are used by Americans, too, often without any idea of their history. *Hobson-Jobson*'s authors spent fourteen years compiling their book, and, as Kate Teltscher notes in her introduction to the latest edition, they were in close correspondence with James Murray, the editor of the ten-volume *New English Dictionary* (later to be renamed the *Oxford English Dictionary*). Many of Yule and Burnell's definitions went straight into Murray's masterwork, with the result that there are around five hundred citations of *Hobson-Jobson* in today's *OED*. So transformed has English been by these loaned words from India that it is possible to make a game of it, as two characters (Flora Crewe, an English poet, and Nirad Das, an Indian artist) do in Tom Stoppard's play *Indian Ink*.

FLORA: While having tiffin on the veranda of my bungalow I spilled kedgeree on my dungarees and had to go to the gymkhana in my pajamas looking like a coolie.

DAS: I was buying chutney in the bazaar when a thug escaped from the choky and killed a box-wallah for his loot, creating a hullabaloo and landing himself in the mulligatawny.

FLORA: I went doolally at the durbar and was sent back to Blighty in a dooley feeling rather dikki with a cup of char and a chit for a chotapeg.

DAS: Yes, and the burra sahib who looked so pukka in his topee sent a coolie to the memsahib—

FLORA: No, no. You can't have memsahib *and* sahib, that's cheating—and anyway I've already said coolie.

DAS: I concede, Miss Crewe. You are the Hobson-Jobson champion.

This exchange sounds so much like a quiz show on NPR or BBC Radio 4 that you'd almost expect Peter Sagal or Sandi Toksvig to interrupt them with a scripted joke and points to the winner.

One who is in mufti is assumed to be at ease, but I have observed that English people often seem more at ease in their uniforms. This could be because absolutely no one does uniforms quite like the English, and it starts from early childhood. More than 90 percent of English children wear uniforms to school from age four, and there is broad agreement, crossing political party lines as well as class lines, that uniforms are a good idea. Reasons the English cite for their approval of uniforms include improving discipline and focus, and leveling class distinctions.

Fewer than a quarter of American schools have uniform policies. Those that do are mostly private, or concentrated in larger cities. But uniform policies have been on the rise, subject to heated debate in the United States since the late '90s, when President Clinton suggested that American schools adopt uniforms to improve students' concentration and cut down on conflict and competition over dress. Not everyone agrees that the problems in American schools can be solved so easily. An American social scientist, David Brunsma, who has studied the subject extensively, concluded that instituting uniform policies did not have any significant impact on student attendance or achievement, but was more "analogous to cleaning and brightly painting a deteriorating building."

Americans are less comfortable with the idea of uniforms than the English, and when objecting to them, they often invoke the ideal of defending individual rights to expression. If Americans are so into their individuality, the English might wonder, then why are they so often seen wearing similar jeans and T-shirts? Why does individuality so often translate to informality, even slovenliness? Why do American tourists, who must have heard how much it rains in England, never seem to carry proper raincoats but instead wear disposable plastic ponchos with flimsy hoods, resembling packs of used Kleenex wafting around London in their "fanny packs"? (The English find this locution hilarious because *fanny* is slang for *vagina*, which they astonishingly will also call a woman's *front bottom*—though this at least sounds less confrontational than America's *vajay-jay*. Reference will also be made, even in medical settings, to the *back passage*, which makes the anus sound like the hallway of a gracious country house—at any rate, somewhere you would be welcome to enter only if you were quite friendly with the family. Incidentally, the English call fanny packs "bum bags," but they hardly ever wear them.) It would seem that Americans, having spent their childhoods in mufti, grow up to adopt a kind of uniform, at least when traveling. But growing up in uniform is certainly no guarantee of one's future sartorial sense.

Too much uniform-wearing can have consequences. Those who are indifferent to clothes end up confused about how to dress themselves in mufti. I have a friend whose husband borrows her socks without compunction—they're the right color, so what's the difference? Some English women, perhaps in reaction to being made to wear pinafores—or worse, plus fours—well into their adolescence, throw modesty to the wind when they at last gain control of their closets. At the first sign of spring, acres of sunburned cleavage and fake-baked legs are revealed, prompting fashion police to decree: "Legs *or* tits out—not both!" Even covering up can be fraught with peril. Although the weather often warrants wearing black opaque tights year-round, they do look out of place in July. And one fashion blogger quipped, while watching the royal wedding, that England ought to have a Ministry of Silly Hats. The peach potty seat Princess Beatrice perched on her head was surely an attention-grabber, but even a cursory look at *HELLO!* magazine in summer would show it was not wholly unrepresentative of what you'd see at a society wedding or Ladies' Day at Ascot. This kind of audacity is one of my favorite things about England. Where an American might play it safe and go for "appropriate," the English are bold with their fashion.

Those who are not indifferent to clothes move on from their natty uniforms to become some of the most flamboyant and imaginative dressers around. There is a brand of confidence that comes from knowing the rules well enough to flout them.

English men, in particular, can be peacocks, fond of hats, uproariously patterned waistcoats (pronounced "weskits"), silk socks, and even the occasional ascot ("askit," please, as if you had to ask it). The American analogue is the exception that proves the rule: the New England preppy. American men who grow up wearing prep school uniforms become the most likely to wear red trousers or needlepoint belts with whale motifs in adult life. Still, the preppy's pink-and-green plumage has a youthful, carefree, and casual spirit about it, and it's primarily an off-duty look.

In England, one can still buy shirts with detachable collars, a style that was invented in America by a housewife who wanted to cut down on her laundry but now is seen as foppish and retro in the extreme. Speaking of foppish and retro, I recently ran into a friend who was carrying a tall cardboard box. He told me he was on his way to drop off his top hat for refurbishment. This did not seem to be a euphemism for anything. It was, he informed me, the best of his top hats. He owns two more: a collapsible one that fits under his seat at the opera, and a "casual" one for outdoor events where he might be sprayed with champagne when someone's horse, or boat, wins. He was frankly put out at the prospect of doing without it for any amount of time. One could not make this up. But believe me, if there is any place this would still be happening in 2015, it is England.

We arrive at Anne's nursery, where most of the mothers are wearing near-identical skinny jeans, neutral cashmere sweaters, ballet flats, and long scarves, wrapped twice. When mufti itself becomes a uniform, we are right back where we started.

Gobsmacked

*In which the English creative class appears to take over
the American media, bringing new slang with it.*

Every so often, a word comes along that means just what
it sounds like. It may not be onomatopoetic, but even if
you've never heard it before, you instantly get the idea.
Gobsmacked is such a word. It means, figuratively, to be flabber-
gasted, amazed, or astounded. Literally, it means to be smacked
in the mouth, as in the song "Gobsmacked" by Chumbawamba
("Outside the pub / Smack you in the gob / Get four long years /
in Wormwood Scrubs").

Gob has been slang for *mouth* in the north of England since
the late 1500s. There are few adjectives that make you look the
way you feel quite like *gobsmacked*. People who say it have to drop
their jaws twice, like large-mouthed bass. You can't use it insin-
cerely; it conveys a certain authenticity. Highly descriptive and

irresistible to many, it is popular as a business name: Gob-smackedMedia, Gobsmacked Records, Gobsmack.tv. It is also a nail polish color (charcoal grey with flecks of glitter from Butter London) and, perhaps most appropriately, a brand of sports mouth guards. It's truth in advertising, mate. Wear it so you don't lose your teeth when you get smacked in the you-know-where.

Not everyone approves of *gobsmacked*. It is a word some associate with cheap tabloid newspapers and oiks from the north. In *The Dictionary of Disagreeable English*, Robert Hartwell Fiske criticizes it as "one of the least attractive words in the English language today." Those who dislike it often come across as a bit priggish and sour. If there is something indelicate about this back-formation, Americans don't care. They are too busy using it every chance they get. But how did *gobsmacked* go from a semi-obscure regionalism in northern England and Scotland in the 1950s, not showing up in the OED until 1987, to international ubiquity?

The word has been common parlance on English TV shows like *Coronation Street*, England's longest-running soap, for decades. Through television, it spread to southern England, where most of the English media are based. *Gobsmacked* began to appear in print around 1985 (according to the *OED*, first in *The Guardian*), and its spread through the UK was soon complete. But this Britishism had yet to take Manhattan. Some commentators date Americans' increasing use of *gobsmacked* to Susan Boyle's star turn on *Britain's Got Talent* in 2009. The self-described "cat lady" from Scotland wiped the smug smirk off Simon Cowell's face with her pitch-perfect performance of "I Dreamed a Dream" from *Les Misérables*. Her performance went viral, and she described herself as "gobsmacked" in dozens of interviews in the days that followed. Still, I believe there is more to the story.

England and America have always traded slang. When America was young, and Anglophobia was strong, Americans resented any incursion. There was a drive to distance American from British English. Noah Webster's 1806 *Compendious Dictionary of the English Language* (the predecessor to his more authoritative and complete 1828 *American Dictionary of the English Language*) was America's first. It was a political document, an attempt to enshrine American independence through language, and to introduce uniform spellings for the first time. Webster's essay "On the Education of Youth in America" left no one in doubt of his position:

> Americans, unshackle your minds, and act like independent beings. You have been children long enough, subject to the control and subservient to the interest of a haughty parent. You have now an interest of your own . . . an empire to raise and support by your exertions, and a national character to establish and extend by your wisdom and virtues. To effect these great objects, it is necessary to frame a liberal plan of policy, and build it on a broad system of education. Before this system can be formed and embraced, the Americans must *believe*, and *act* from the belief, that it is dishonorable to waste life in mimicking the follies of other nations and basking in the sunshine of foreign glory.

Webster's *American Spelling Book*, also known as the "Blue Backed Speller," was one of America's earliest bestselling books, providing American children with a moral and academic educa-

tion for more than 160 years and reinforcing the spelling re-
forms (*colour* became *color*, *theatre* became *theater*, *oesophagus*
became *esophagus*, etc.) that are among the most lasting aspects
of Webster's legacy. America's beloved spelling bees are another,
taking place at every level from the smallest classroom in the re-
motest corner of the country to the national contest, which is
televised. Americans have a history of being territorial about
their language, and it continues today, though England's slang is
the least of their worries. Now that Americans have established
their national character, they find English slang charming, if always a little pretentious, regardless of a word's original class
connotations in England. Americans still love to think of themselves as uncorrupted by such things, but Ben Yagoda, an author
and professor of English at the University of Delaware, tracks
the progress of NOOBs (Not One-Off Britishisms)—traditionally
British expressions that have been widely adopted in the United
States—and he never runs out of material.

Meanwhile, in England, one sees articles with headlines
like "Top Ten Most Annoying Americanisms." Matthew Engel,
in a BBC article titled "Why Do Some Americanisms Irritate
People?," neatly captured the anxiety over American influence
with a militaristic metaphor: "What the world is speaking—
even on levels more sophisticated than basic Globish—is not
necessarily our English. According to the *Oxford Guide to World
English*, 'American English has a global role at the beginning of
the 21st Century comparable to that of British English at the
start of the 20th.' The alarming part is that this is starting to
show in the language we speak in Britain. American usages no
longer swim to our shores as single spies, as 'reliable' and 'talented' did. They come in battalions."

So eager are the bashers of Americanisms that Americans are often unjustly blamed for neologisms that actually emanated from the other side of the Atlantic. For example, it's easy to find an English or a French person who enjoys eating eggs and pancakes at eleven thirty in the morning, but it's hard to find one who will countenance the word *brunch* (or worse: *le brunch*). Yet *brunch* did not originate in America. An Englishman, Guy Beringer, coined this portmanteau word back in 1896. Surprisingly, the concept of the all-you-can-drink brunch was *not* invented by the English, but was an American innovation. No one in England has yet complained about the spread of this concept to their shores.

The English used to complain bitterly (and some still do) about the steady encroachment of Americanisms into their language via television, film, and advertising. But one could argue that these days, the crossover is about equal. This is because of the preponderance of English journalists, editors, and television producers who have infiltrated America at the highest levels of their professions.

The current CEO of *The New York Times* and the editor of the New York *Daily News* are English. So are the presidents of ABC and NBC News and the editors of American *Vogue* and *Cosmopolitan*. Reality television is dominated by a few British producers, like Mark Burnett (*Survivor*, *The Apprentice*, *The Voice*) and Simon Cowell (*The X Factor*, *American Idol*). Tina Brown, Piers Morgan, and the late Christopher Hitchens, among others, have had an undeniable influence on highbrow American pop culture. Although England's population is one-sixth the size of the United States', it supports more than a dozen national newspapers. (America has only three, and many would argue that *USA Today* hardly counts.) "The British news media market is a brutal and competitive crucible; it breeds frankness, excellence and a fair amount of excess. In that context, American journalism's historical values of objectivity and fairness seem quaint." For proof, look no further than the difference between the BBC's aggressive—even combative—interview style versus the more subdued NPR approach. English journalists have a tendency to go for the jugular, and Americans find it refreshing. For now. Is it any wonder that English slang has become incredibly fashionable? Noah Webster would be gobsmacked.

Trainers

In which America and England are shown to be among the world's fattest countries, despite their apparent dedication to fitness.

As countries with obesity rates of 34 percent and 25 percent, respectively, the United States and the United Kingdom might be supposed to be less than obsessed with fitness. But the sad truth is that two of the top five fat-ass nations worldwide have fitness industries worth more than thirty-two billion dollars combined. About half of adults in England and America "take exercise," as the English say, making it sound like doctor's orders. (And in many cases, it is.) But some people actually *really* enjoy it. And it's those people I'm going to talk about here, since I'm sure they are sick of hearing how slothful their nations are when they are out there lacing up their sneakers—for fun—every day.

In England, sneakers or running shoes are called *trainers*. A fact I am never allowed to forget, because my four-year-old is bilingual. The other day I heard her say to a friend, "I am putting on my trainers. My mummy calls them *sneakers*, because she is American." (At least she has stopped correcting my English to my face, which is the last thing I want to hear when we're trying to get out the door in the morning.) In America, trainers are private fitness instructors who bludgeon you into shape with your consent. England has private fitness coaches, too, though most people who can afford them are still more likely to spend on a good bottle of wine or a haircut than an hour in the gym.

Gyms are less popular in England than they are in America. Although, as Emma Sinclair wrote in the *Telegraph*, some American boutique gyms are moving into the English market with "responsive customer service . . . and faultless facilities that create customer loyalty and . . . leave a wake of grey UK gyms in their trail." Not all the gyms in England are gray and uninspiring, but many of them do feel like a time warp to 1998. Step aerobics is still a going concern. SoulCycle arrived in London in 2014—eight years after it first caught on in New York. Ballet barre classes and Pilates are still a bit rarefied, and haven't reached saturation point in gyms around the country. CrossFit is gaining in reputation, but it will take years to build the following it enjoys in America. When I first moved to London, a Google search for "yoga London" turned up fewer than five dedicated studios. The small New Hampshire town where my in-laws live has seven.

Americans are very faddish about exercise—so much so that it's easy to forget that the American obsession with fitness is fairly new. It wasn't until the late 1970s that strenuous exercise became something ordinary people—not just "health nuts"—did. It's telling that Americans often speak of exercise in terms that other cultures reserve for their spiritual practices. They flock to exercise "gurus" who promise enlightenment along with a high calorie burn. They are "religious" about their workouts. Some fitness classes or instructors acquire a "cultlike" following and are spoken of with reverence not usually accorded to people who get paid by the hour. Americans love their gyms—and not just because extreme weather and unwalkable suburbs make outside exercise difficult in many places. They are joiners and appreciate the social aspects of a shared workout experience.

The English are more likely to head outside for their exercise. Whether they love or hate it, outdoor exercise is a huge part of childhood in England. While schools in America are canceling recess and dropping their PE programs, English schools are fanatical about games, and about getting children outside in all weather. A rhyme often repeated to young children in shorts, as their knees turn blue, is "Whether the weather be fine, Or whether the weather be not / Whether the weather be cold, Or whether the weather be hot / We'll weather the weather / Whatever the weather / Whether we like it or not!" There is pride in stoicism when it comes to outdoor exercise—it's one of the last vestiges of the English stiff upper lip. Even if it has been raining for three consecutive days and the playing fields are knee-deep in mud, the football (soccer) practice won't be canceled. It would be a bad precedent to set. When would the lads ever play? Parents huddle on the sidelines with flasks of tea (maybe something stronger) and wait it out.

As adults, the English remain far more willing than Americans to exercise in the muck. Witness the popularity of British

Military Fitness—the UK's ubiquitous outdoor fitness classes: "the best way to get fitter, faster, stronger and have fun whilst doing so." (Am I the only one who finds the priggish "whilst" hilarious in this context?) Any day of the year, in parks across the country you will see people in multicolored bibs—blue for beginners, red for intermediates, and green for advanced—huffing and puffing through press-ups (push-ups), burpees, and shuttle runs, while being shouted at by buff former soldiers. America has "boot camp" style workouts, too, but they usually take place inside temperature-controlled gyms.

Fit or not, most people in England share a love of their unspoiled countryside. Green Belt legislation has restricted urban sprawl, so that within minutes by car or train of any town or city (even London) one can reach—instead of strip malls and big-box stores as far as the eye can see—unbroken stretches of walkable land. Even where homes and farms exist, rights of way—paths where members of the public have a legal right to pass—are protected. The Ordnance Survey, which maintains the definitive record of every geographical feature in Great Britain, publishes 650 different maps of every corner of the country. Although customizable maps are available free on their website www.ordnance survey.co.uk, they still sell around 2.5 million paper maps each year—a testament to England's devotion to country walking.

Combining this love of the countryside with a certain masochistic pleasure is the sport of fell running, or trail running, which originated in the mountainous regions of northern England. Basically, it is running straight up and down mountains. In an interview with the *Telegraph*, Richard Askwith, author of *Feet in the Clouds: A Tale of Fell-Running and Obsession*, said the sport "reconnects you with the most basic of your instincts:

the survival instinct, for example. Running down a rocky mountain at speed is dangerous, but that is what is so attractive: the chance to throw off the caution most of us live with most of the time and feel free again." Askwith completed the Bob Graham Round, a fell run comprising ascents and descents of forty-two peaks, in twenty-four hours—a distance of seventy miles and total climbs of twenty-seven thousand feet, saying that "there would be no sense of satisfaction without the pain." He considers himself an amateur, by the way.

Perhaps it isn't surprising that the Tough Mudder races were invented by two Englishmen—Will Dean and Guy Livingstone. Their first races were held in America, where it took them just three years to find one million people willing to leave their gyms behind, if only for a day, and put themselves through their punishing, British Special Forces–designed obstacle courses, which are ten to twelve miles long and include freezing swims (the "arctic enema"), narrow pipes full of mud (the "boa constrictor"), and electric shocks, in case the course isn't harrowing enough. The races have since expanded internationally, including to England. Participants get the satisfaction of a race completed, but they also raise money for veterans charities.

The English are far more willing to take on a physical challenge if they have a charity fund-raising goal in mind. I have never met an English person who planned to run a marathon, jump out of an airplane, or take part in a 150-mile footrace through the Sahara Desert in one-hundred-degree heat without first asking friends and family to pony up for a cause. There is a sense that taking on a grueling training schedule is rather selfish and solipsistic and that one needs to offset that somehow. Needless to say, pushy slogans and lifestyle branding are not their thing. Americans also raise money for charity by performing feats of athletic prowess, but they are more ego-driven and likely to see training for such events as virtuous in itself.

For a sense of how much individualism and self-actualization motivates Americans, look no further than the US Army's recent recruitment slogans. For years it was "Be all that *you* can be"—emphasizing the individual over the group, even though there are not many jobs more communal and team-oriented than being a soldier. Recent army slogans have taken the theme even further: "An army of one" and "Defy expectations." The British Army's slogan, "Be the best," doesn't address the individual at all, and the Royal Navy's is simply "This team works." The desire to do something like run a marathon purely for the sake of achieving a "personal best" time or proving to themselves that they can do it doesn't embarrass Americans. Neither does being told by a clothing company to "Do one thing every day that scares you!" For the English, listening to an American talk about his health and fitness regimen just might qualify.

Sorry

*In which we find out why the English refuse to apologize
for their overuse of* sorry.

A recent survey concluded that the average English
person will say *sorry* more than 1.9 million times in
his lifetime. This may strike some as a conservative
estimate. From this, one could deduce that the English are especially polite. This might be true if *sorry* were always, or even
usually, a straightforward apology. It isn't. The reason they stay
on the sorry-go-round is that the word, in their English, is so
very versatile. A. A. Gill, writing for the benefit of visitors to the
London Olympics, bragged, "Londoners are just permanently
petulant, irritated. I think we wake up taking offense. All those
English teacup manners, the exaggerated please and thank
yous, are really the muzzle we put on our short tempers. There

are, for instance, a dozen inflections of the word sorry. Only one of them means 'I'm sorry.' "

Here are just a few of the many moods and meanings these two syllables can convey:

> "Sorry!" (I stepped on your foot.)
>
> "Sorry." (You stepped on my foot.)
>
> "Sorry?" (I didn't catch what you just said.)
>
> "SOrry." (You are an idiot.)
>
> "SORRY." (Get out of my way.)
>
> "SorRY." (The nerve of some people!)
>
> "I'm sorry but . . ." (Actually I'm not at all.)
>
> "Sorry . . ." (I can't help you.)

It's all in the tone, of course, and this is where *sorry* becomes permanently lost in translation. An American friend will never forget when she finally figured out that *sorry* can be a tool of passive aggression in England's hierarchical social system—a form of dismissal. When she was a college kid in England and people gave her an apology that was not sincere, but meant to put her in her place, she would respond earnestly, "Oh, no, it's okay! Don't worry!" Why wouldn't she? There are times when luck favors the ignorant.

The English have a reputation for being passive-aggressive because they seem not to be saying what they mean—at least, not with words. In English culture, an anodyne word like *sorry* takes on shades of meaning that someone from outside will not be able to discern with any degree of sophistication, especially if he is from a culture that is more comfortable with confrontation, or one that condones a wider range of small talk among strangers. The English use *sorry* to protest, to ask you to repeat yourself, to soothe, and to smooth over social awkwardness as much as—if not more than—they use it to apologize. But most of the time, their object is politeness of a particularly English kind, to wit: politeness as refusal.

English courtesy often takes the form of what sociolinguists Penelope Brown and Stephen C. Levinson have called "negative politeness"—which depends on keeping a respectful distance from others and not imposing on them. Its opposite, positive politeness, is inclusive and assumes others' desire for our approval.

Only the Japanese—masters of negative politeness—have anything even approaching the English *sorry* reflex. No wonder visiting Americans are so often caught off guard, and so often feel they've been the objects of passive aggression or dismissal instead of politeness. Their misunderstanding of what constitutes politeness in England is not surprising, since Americans epitomize positive politeness.

When Americans say *sorry*, they mostly mean it. But, at least to English ears, they don't necessarily mean anything else they say. Americans repeat seemingly empty phrases like "Have a nice day!" They also give and receive compliments easily, even among strangers. The English find this behavior highly suspect. Hence, the American reputation for insincerity.

The English novelist Patricia Finney has said that she loves Americans because "it doesn't matter whether people actually respect me or not, so long as they treat me with courtesy and respect . . . I really don't mind if nice American check-out guys tell me to have a nice day and are really thinking, 'hope you have a terrible day, you snotty Brit,' so long as I don't know about it. I think sincerity is over-rated in any case." Americans don't. Americans prize sincerity above most qualities. (How else are they going to ensure that the Great Pumpkin picks their patch?) An American friend of Finney's accordingly defended the practice, saying Americans ". . . do respect people. It's not faked."

It could be that Americans have stopped hearing themselves. Just like the English with their *sorries*, they have certainly stopped expecting a response. Imagine the shock of a salesman who said, "Have a nice day!" to the grandfather of a friend, who answered, "Thank you, but I have other plans."

Americans are sociable and approval-seeking. They look for common ground with others and genuinely want to connect. This often takes the form of compliments—especially to complete strangers. ("I really like your wapdoodle!" "What a great snockticker!") This is because American society's fluidity can lead to insecurity. Your place in the hierarchy is based not on who you *are*, but what you *do* (and how much you *make*). Therefore, Americans incessantly seek reassurance that they are doing all right. But the marvelous thing is that they also seek to give reassurance. That may be the quality that Finney was responding to.

In English culture, you're assumed to be secure in your place, to know where you stand. But in real life, who does? Practically no one. *Sorry* and American compliments serve similar social purposes. When there's nothing to say, we can avoid social awkwardness and either deflect (UK) or connect (USA)—all in the name of politeness. *Sorry* simultaneously avoids confrontation and, when used sincerely, allows people to show how lovely they are, *really*, despite their minor transgressions. American compliments allow for a little connection, and reinforce your belonging on a level that's comfortable—at least if you're American.

Either way, you're left with something to say, and on that note, Jane Austen will have the last word on *sorry*. Here she is in a letter to her elder sister:

My dearest Cassandra

My expectation of having nothing to say to you after the conclusion of my last, seems nearer Truth than I thought it would be, for I feel to have but little . . . you may accordingly prepare for my ringing the Changes of the Glads and Sorrys for the rest of the page.—Unluckily, however, I see nothing to be glad of, unless I make it a matter of Joy that Mrs. Wylmot has another son and that Lord Lucan has taken a Mistress, both of which Events are of course joyful to the Actors;—but to be sorry I find many occasions, the first is that your return is to be delayed, & whether I ever get beyond the first is doubtful. It is no use to lament.—I never heard that even Queen Mary's Lamentation did her any good, & I could not therefore expect benefit from mine.—We are all sorry, & now that subject is exhausted.

Toilet

*In which we attempt to bring back a useful old word
(while simultaneously discouraging
the use of a vulgar one).*

Everyone has a private list of least-favorite words. Words that we shrink from using, and cringe to hear. They are like dog whistles, emitting a high and excruciating frequency audible only to us, while others go blissfully about their business. The renowned American gastronome M. F. K. Fisher, writing about her own opinions, prejudices, and aversions, used the antiquated Scottish noun *scunner*. Where has this useful word gone? Certainly the human race has only become less tolerant since her essay "As the Lingo Languishes" was published in 1980. These days, we take scunners against people, places, and things all the time. There ought to be a meme.

Fisher held scunners against the words *yummy* and *scrumptious* because, she said, "there is no dignity in such infantile evasions of plain words like *good*." Just because a scunner can be explained doesn't mean it is rational. There is something a bit primal, or at least involuntary, about these antipathies. The word *succulent* makes me want to go hide in a closet and never come out. No idea why.

Scunners can be highly personal, even secret to all but the closest of friends. Scunners can also be ferociously tribal. A shared scunner can unite individuals like little else. If you doubt it, dare to Google a word such as *moist*, which may, to you, seem entirely innocent. Or you may just have flung this book to the floor in disgust. Either way, you might be interested to know that several pieces of fairly serious journalism are dedicated to explaining the scunner against the *m* word, which is apparently widespread. Its haters have their own Facebook group.

It's rare that a scunner crosses nationalities, but we have a winner in *toilet*. It is generally, though by no means universally, unloved on both sides of the moist, moist Atlantic. Neither the Americans nor the English like to say the word *toilet*, and not just because of the diphthong it shares with the *m* word: *oi*. (Oy.)

Americans, who love to accuse the English of prissiness, are a bit prissy themselves. No less an authority than *The Economist* has pointed out that "bodily functions . . . seem to embarrass Americans especially: one can ask for the 'loo' in a British restaurant without budging an eyebrow; don't try that in New York." In America, euphemism is such big business that even doctors and nurses will say someone "passed" instead of "died." Roosters are rarely cocks. American trash goes to a landfill. Its elderly (never "old") pets are "put to sleep." And Americans use the "bathroom" at home or "restroom" when out in public. Even "restroom" is too much for the sensibilities of some Americans, who instead go to the "powder room" to "wash their hands."

Americans have been accused, with some justification, of being more Victorian than the Victorians. In fact, Noah Webster's purified Bible, in which he substituted euphemisms for words he judged potentially "offensive to delicacy," predated Queen Victoria's coronation. On Webster's watch, *fornication* became *lewdness, piss* became *excretions*, and *stink* was replaced by *odious*. Americans never want to offend. There's a mania for putting the best face on everything, and avoiding the inelegant. It's all terribly middle-class.

Bizarrely, this is where *toilet* prejudice began in England. The upper and lower classes historically had little use for euphemisms. As landowners or tenant farmers, they were in constant contact with birth, death, and excrement. At least in theory. It was the striving middle, in their desire to disassociate from the working class, who started prettying up their language by using French words like *toilette*, which the upper class cannot abide.

As Philip Thody explains in *Don't Do It! A Dictionary of the Forbidden*, "The landed aristocracy shares with its tenants a suspicion of foreign habits which is reflected in its preference for Anglo-Saxon over Latin terms. Members of the English upper class say *chop* and not *cutlet* . . . *jam* and not *preserves*, *pudding* and not *dessert* . . ." Upper-class avoidance of supposedly refined language has created many linguistic taboos. Thus *toilet*, which would seem to be about as direct and uneuphemistic as any word can be, came into use as an affectation of the petty bourgeoisie and is still seen that way. The affected have ever been the objects of scorn and ridicule (like the snobbish,

status-obsessed Hyacinth Bucket—pronounced *Bouquet*—on
the BBC series *Keeping Up Appearances*).

It is hard to believe that antipathy to *toilet* lingers when many
class markers in language have gone the way of the dodo, and
every public convenience in England has a sign saying TOILET in
one-thousand-point type. Maybe that's part of the problem. It
makes *toilet* seem all the more common, and those who say it
even more so. In her book *The Anglo Files: A Field Guide to the
British*, Sarah Lyall avers that *toilet* is considered by many "a virtual profanity, the biggest class marker of all." She quotes a
woman who told the *Guardian* writer Jonathan Margolis, "I'd
rather my children said *fuck* than *toilet*."

The English find American linguistic hedges rather droll—
especially *bathroom* when used for public conveniences because, as they love to point out, "There is no bath in there!"—but
they have their own in *loo* and *lavatory*. *Lavatory* comes straight
from the Christian church, and refers to the ritual washing of
the celebrant's hands at the offertory. You can't get much cleaner
than that. Going to the "lavatory" is one of the humorously in-
congruous things Monty Python's singing lumberjack does,
along with poncing around the shops every Wednesday, having
"buttered scones for tea," and cross-dressing.

If you are an anxious American who wishes neither to offend
nor come across as common, *lavatory* is considered unimpeach-
able. It is the *restroom* of English English. The origins of *loo* are
unknown but vaguely, possibly French. This doesn't make it suspect, exactly, but it's less formal—the word to use at someone's
house if you don't already know where you're going. Of course, if
you don't give a shit what anyone thinks, you know what word
you can use.

Cheers

In which we find out why Queen Victoria said, "Give my people plenty of beer, good beer, and cheap beer, and you will have no revolution among them."

Pubs have occupied a privileged place in English social life since Anglo-Saxon times, and although their number peaked in 1869, and many have closed in recent years, there are still more than fifty-seven thousand pubs in Britain. In his prewar love letter to pubs, *The Local*, Maurice Gorham explains one of the reasons pubs are so beloved, and why they endure. "Every pub is somebody's local, and every one has its regulars . . . You see them ensconced in the corner by the partition, deep in conversation with the landlady when you come in . . . The real regular is one of the family. . . . As a regular myself, I have heard more about the affairs of licensed houses than I know about any of my friends . . . Nothing much is demanded of the regular except to come regularly and show himself interested in the pub's affairs. He need not even drink very much."

Practically every town, every neighborhood, in England has a pub fitting this description, which will bring to the American mind nothing so much as reruns of *Cheers*, a thirty-year-old television show that took place in an idealized local bar "where everybody knows your name." America has no analogue to the pub—at least not as a national institution. Americans romanticize English pubs because they tend to drink in anonymous sports bars and chain restaurants with wall-mounted televisions, rather than fireplaces or polished wooden bars, as their focal points. Those lucky enough to have a charming local of their own don't take it for granted, as much of the country makes do with TGI Fridays and Chili's. (Although, to be fair, I haven't yet found a pub snack that can compare to Chili's Boneless Buffalo Wings.)

Although Americans and the English have different drinking customs and habits, *cheers* has been used as a toast in both countries for nearly a century. It comes from the Old French *chiere*, meaning *face*. *Cheer* later came to mean an expression or mood, and later a good mood. In England by the mid-1970s, *cheers* had become a colloquial synonym for *thanks*. *Cheers* has been used that way by the English ever since, and is a remarkably flexible word. It is, for one thing, a great class leveler: Practically everyone says it, and it is appropriate to say to anyone (with the possible exception of the queen, and yet the younger royals surely use it). *Cheers* can also mean *good-bye* and is the simplest thing to say at the end of any small transaction, not just at the pub but at the newsagent, getting out of a taxi, or when someone has done you a small favor. It's as friendly and warm as the pub itself.

Perhaps because of pubs, social life in England revolves around drinking to a greater extent than it does in America. English journalist Lucy Foster, who undertook a month of sobriety as an assignment for *Stylist* magazine, said, "There's a rule of thumb within my friendship group . . . that you can't trust people who don't drink . . . They're questionable. They have issues, dark secrets, or a health agenda." Alcohol's great appeal is that it "makes you talk and it makes you share, and it makes you feel good, if only for a little while." After her harrowing account of her teetotal January, and skeptical interviews with a recovering alcoholic and a man who is sober for religious reasons, a box titled "The Sober Truth" asks, ominously, "After four weeks without a drop of alcohol, how do Lucy's relationships fare?" (The short answer: Poorly.)

There has been a lot of hand-wringing over binge drinking in the UK in recent years, for good reason. An American friend who has lived in both countries summed it up: "The public health definition of 'binge drinking' in the USA is something like 'having five drinks at one sitting.' In the UK it's something like 'remaining intoxicated for 48 straight hours.'" Like most exaggerations, it contains a grain of truth: In the United States, five or more drinks in one sitting *is* considered a binge. In the UK, you're looking at an eight-drink minimum. In his book *The English Pub*, Peter Haydon includes a telling bit of doggerel: "Not drunk is he who from the floor / Can rise again and still drink more. / But drunk is he who prostrate lies / Without the power to drink or rise." But anxiety about drink has never dampened enthusiasm for the pub.

Two prints by William Hogarth, *Beer Street* and *Gin Lane*, published in 1751, tell a story that has changed little in the past two and a half centuries. Hogarth made the prints in support of a campaign directed against gin drinking among London's poor. *Beer Street* is a wholesome scene that celebrates the virtues of England's traditional drink. The subjects of this print are the well-fed, industrious, and prosperous middle class. *Gin Lane* is an altogether different place. The subjects of this print are malnourished and debauched. A carpenter sells his tools to buy gin. A mother drops her baby over a railing. A body is crammed into a coffin. The message is that drinking is not bad in itself; it's excessive drinking, especially by the lower classes, that is the problem. In 1751, the aim was to stop sales of small amounts of cheap and highly intoxicating gin in local shops, to make it less accessible. There has been talk of instituting a per-unit minimum price to limit consumption of the alcohol available in supermarkets, with their ubiquitous three-for-two offers.

Irresponsible drinking costs the UK taxpayer twenty-one billion pounds per year if you count extra police presence and medical bills. The British Medical Association estimates that nearly a quarter of the population drinks to excess. The most convincing argument against minimum pricing is that it amounts to a tax on the poor, when it is the higher-income groups, undeterred by the price of a decent pinot, that have seen the largest rises in alcohol consumption.

American consumption rivals that of the English, and causes the same kinds of social problems. But America is a much more religious country and there is shame associated with most pleasurable activities, especially drinking. Although Prohibition was repealed in 1933, some local communities opted to keep its strict regulations against public drinking in place, with the result that today there are still more than two hundred dry counties in America, and many more that are partially dry. Most of these counties are located in a single swath of the Bible Belt, but there are outliers. Pennsylvania, Ohio, and Michigan all have strict enough laws in most of their counties to qualify as partially dry, and even in liberal New England, deep in the heart of Cheever country, where WASP reserve requires some dousing of its own, there are still dry towns.

America has always been more conservative and less relaxed than England when it comes to drinking. In 1832, Frances Trollope (mother of Anthony) came to America to seek her fortune and ended up writing a book about American manners instead. She wrote, "We [English] are by no means so gay as our lively neighbours on the other side of the channel, but, compared with Americans, we are whirligigs and tetotums [spinning tops]; everyday is a holyday, and every night a festival." American attitudes to drinking vary by region. Whereas in Brooklyn a two-year-old's birthday party could be held at a beer garden, eyebrows might go up in Albany, and in some cities you'd actually be breaking the law. Many Americans avoid drinking for health reasons, without the same stigma that this carries in England. And as much as Californians, for example, love their local wine, they have to be careful not to run afoul of ever-stricter drunk driving laws. On the other hand, drive-through liquor stores were certainly an American invention, and are dotted all around the South, near some of the same areas where regulations are most stringent. Americans are conflicted drinkers, to say the least.

Prohibitionists once advocated punishments for drinkers, including giving them poisoned alcoholic beverages, banishing them to concentration camps in the Aleutian Islands, branding, whipping, sterilizing, and even executing them. Is it any wonder that, fewer than one hundred years later, American attitudes to drinking have not recovered? What would the purists say if they knew that "The Star-Spangled Banner" was written to the tune of an old drinking song?

This is why Americans envy English pubs. Pubs are safe and friendly places where everyone is made to feel welcome. You can have lunch, bring your kids (at least during the day). Visiting Americans might find the mixed drinks a bit stingy, due to strict standardization of measures (twenty-five to thirty-five milliliters is the maximum legal serving of spirits), but one could argue this is a public service, given the well-documented perils of gin. The beer is much more interesting anyway. For their part, the English in America might be surprised by the quality of American beer. Craft breweries are proliferating and giving the drinking public options beyond the very cold, very bland national brands in cans. They would be less impressed by the mixed drinks served in American bars, heavily iced and inevitably containing straws, which no English person over the age of five would be caught dead using.

Where does this leave *cheers*? Perhaps because of visits to England, or the influence of English novels, television, and journalism, Americans have begun to adopt the "thanks/good-bye" meaning of late. As one American said, "I enjoy hearing [cheers] instead of the worn out 'later' or 'see ya later.' Like it or not, the Yanks and the Brits are cousins, and that's that. Cheers!" Needless to say, not everyone shares his enthusiasm.

An English banker living in New York groused, "I'm getting sick of my clients saying *cheers* to me. Americans say *cheers* like Dick Van Dyke in *Mary Poppins*, with too much enthusiasm. It must be delivered laconically." Delivery does count. The English say "Chis" out of the sides of their mouths when they mean *thank you* or *good-bye*. Americans do not pick up on this, and say *cheers* the same—toothily, hitting the *r* a bit hard and implying an exclamation point—whether they mean it as a toast or a casual good-bye. Some Americans are just as irritated by their compatriots' appropriation of *cheers*. One ranted, "Why is everyone saying *cheers* these days? . . . I am going to start saying . . . 'Did I just have a drink and not know it?' "

The backlash against Americans who borrow *cheers* may seem churlish, but it wouldn't surprise a linguist. As M. Lynne Murphy wrote in her blog, "Separated by a Common Language," "If you're using words from a different place that you don't have 'birth rights' to, you're seen as 'inauthentic' in the use of those words . . . as aspiring to be associated with a group of people who may not always be positively stereotyped in the culture you're in—and those stereotypes rub off on your word usage . . . So, taking on American words is seen as 'sloppy' and 'lazy' in the UK. Taking on British words is seen as 'snobby' and 'pretentious' in the US."

There is only one way this could end: Cheers.

Knackered

In which our children arrive to
collectively lobotomize us.

E ven if you had no idea what *knackered* meant, you couldn't miss it in context: "I'm absolutely *knackered*." It is English slang for "exhausted," and it usually comes with a certain sag of the shoulders and a little stagger in the voice. There is a particularly English way of saying it, too. Whereas an American might over-egg the *r*—thus sounding far too perky to be knackered—the English elide it. It's pronounced *nnakk-uhd*: slow on the first syllable, swallowing the second.

But *exhausted* doesn't quite capture the full sense of *knackered*. The knacker's yard is, literally, an abattoir for horses that have outlived their ability to stand, run, and carry. The *Oxford English Dictionary* puts an even finer point on it with this definition of the verb *to knacker*: "to kill; to castrate; usu. in weakened sense, to exhaust, to wear out." The examples that follow are of athletes and soldiers. But in my experience, "I'm knack-ered" is the new parents' refrain.

Becoming a parent in an adopted country is one of the best assimilation exercises there is. The shared experiences of pregnancy and early parenthood give you the opportunity to meet, and get to know, people with whom you may have had little in common before you popped your sprogs. (That's English English for before your babies arrived.) You end up on maternity wards, in baby classes and playgroups and Internet chat rooms, with people whose vocabulary for this phase of life is entirely foreign. You can't help but learn almost as many new words as your *bub* (baby).

First you are initiated into the medical system, with its ac-ronyms and quirks. In England the NHS (National Health Service) assures every pregnant woman a good basic standard of care in a public hospital, free of charge (or at least covered by taxes). Beyond that, the NHS provides each woman with extra care as needed. In practice this means that if you have a problem, you get all the attention you need; otherwise, very little indeed. Anyone experiencing an uncomplicated pregnancy under the NHS feels lucky, if a bit neglected. The standard number of ultrasounds for an NHS pregnancy is two—not the half dozen that a well-insured American would expect. But on the other hand, *everyone* gets two. No one is left out of prenatal care entirely, which still happens in America. And even the best-insured Americans do not walk out of the hospital postdelivery owing nothing. During my entire NHS pregnancy and birth, I was asked to pay a grand total of £2.50. That was for the printout of my second ultrasound. Those who want more personalized care can choose to see a private doctor and deliver in a private hospital. It will cost you or your insurance company about £15,000—about the same, or a bit less, than the average cost in the United States.

After the NHS, the most important acronym for English parents is the NCT (National Childbirth Trust). This organization operates as a charity with two main purposes: to advocate for parents' rights and interests, and to educate new parents. Its bias toward natural, drug-free birth is not entirely uncontroversial—some feel the NCT presents too rosy a picture of what childbirth is actually like, and joke that the acronym really stands for Natural Childbirth Trust. It's hippy-dippy, warm, and welcoming—"crunchy" in a way that wouldn't be out of place in Park Slope or Portland, but isn't usually associated with England.

Still, joining the NCT and taking their *antenatal* (prenatal) classes is a rite of passage for thousands of English parents. The greatest benefit may be community. It is not unusual for tight bonds to form within NCT antenatal groups, lasting long after the maternity leave (usually six months to a year in England) is over and even sometimes after the children have left home. The NCT introduced me to the charmingly old-fashioned custom of bringing cake to each new friend's family as the babies were born, and my NCT group spent so much time together that any of the parents could pick up and comfort any of the others' babies, as if we were one big family. It was a fascinating experience of permeable or nonexistent boundaries that lasted about a year, until the last of us had returned to work.

Not that we weren't busy. We took long walks with our pushchairs and prams (short for *perambulator*, a word that calls to mind nannies in starched white uniforms rather than mummies in tracksuits with tricked-out Bugaboos). We had vigorous debates about whether or not babies should be given dummies (pacifiers), and whether to spring for the chicken pox jab (a vaccine not standard under the NHS) at a private clinic. We exchanged helpful tips on how to get posset (spit-up) stains out of Babygros (onesies). Posset is—confusingly, disgustingly—also the name of a creamy dessert, and many desserts were consumed that year as we fretted over the statistics on cot (crib) death and balanced infants on our knees. We had the camaraderie of trench mates who knew we wouldn't be judged for whinging (whining) or throwing wobblies (tantrums) over our sleeplessness, our partners' lack of understanding, or insensitive comments from the in-laws. Perhaps unsurprisingly, one of the most common acronyms on Mumsnet, England's most popular online forum for mothers, is AIBU ("Am I being unreasonable?"), to which one may respond: YABU or YANBU.

We had a multicultural group. Two-thirds were English, but we had an American (me), an Italian, and an Australian as well. So there were some English words I had to adopt, or no one would know what the hell I was talking about. I fought this a little. My friend George, an Englishman married to an American and raising a family in New York, had the same reaction. We both feel the need to hold on to some of the vocabulary of our own childhoods—not just for our comfort, but so our children will not be entirely assimilated. Just as I could never bring myself to say *nappy*, George could never say *diaper*. But my daughter thwarted my attempt to make her "bilingual" by making up her own words. Diapers became *gagas* by a strange logic: If her father called it a *nappy*, and her babysitter used the French word, *couche*, and Mama said *diaper*, we must all be making up our

own language and therefore she could, too. We all ended up calling it a *gaga* after a while. But that's what a shared cultural experience is all about—whether it's the culture within a country,
a chat room, an NCT group, or a single home.

Once a child hits the toddler years and goes off to nursery
(preschool), the cultural confusion intensifies. American parents in England have to get used to saying *trousers* instead of
pants (underwear), and applying *plasters* or *Elastoplasts* instead of *Band-Aids*. They have to learn that "to go potty" in English English means "to go a bit crazy"—something you would
never invite a toddler to do in an enclosed space. They have to
get used to their children calling the letter *Z zed* and not *zee*,
and zeros being *noughts*—as in, a game of noughts and crosses
instead of tic-tac-toe. And hearing a lie referred to as a *porky*
(this comes from Cockney rhyming slang, in which *porky pies*
stands in for *lies*). Incidentally, when your child asks for *rubbers*
to take to school in year one (kindergarten), don't panic: He
means erasers. And because accents and language tend to be in-
fluenced more by peers than parents, you may be in for a lifetime of being called "Mummy," so by all means, stop picturing
the Egyptian wing of the Met . . . if you can.

Nursery rhymes common to children in both countries have
subtly different lyrics that will strike the American parent as
sacrilegious. The first time your child sings, "Ring around the
rosy, a pocket full of posies, *Atish-oo, Atish-oo*, we all fall down,"
you might stifle the urge to teach her to sing it your way. But
some of the differences will seem like upgrades. The "Hokey
Pokey" will be even funnier as the "Hokey Cokey," and you might
find the chorus of the English version unexpectedly charming:
"Whoa, the hokey cokey / Whoa, the hokey cokey / Whoa, the

hokey cokey / Knees bent, arms stretched, RAH! RAH! RAH!"
With a rousing chorus like that, who wouldn't prefer the "Hokey
Cokey"? The *Telegraph* reported that HRH the Prince of Wales,
on a recent trip to Sri Lanka, walked into a classroom where
children were doing the dance and joined in "bending his knees,
stretching his arms and turning around, clearly enjoying the
chance to 'shake it all about.'" It seems that some pleasures are
universal.

It would be impossible to generalize about differences between American and English parenting styles. There is probably about as much variation in viewpoints and practices between
Islington and Kensington as there is between London and New
York. Yet the experience of parenting young children is much
the same wherever you go: a complete blur.

No wonder everyone is knackered.

Brolly

In which the rain, it raineth. Every. Single. Day.

When the art installation "Rain Room" debuted in London, more than seventy-seven thousand people visited, some waiting for as long as twelve hours to get in. Its creators, a young London-based art collective called rAndom International, described their work as a "hundred square metre field of falling water through which it is possible to walk . . . without being drenched." Motion sensors detected where people stood and stopped the flow of water around them. Many of the visitors in London, and in New York when the exhibit moved to the Museum of Modern Art, had the experience of waiting in the (actual) rain in order to know the sensation of controlling the (artificial) rain. rAndom International is made up of eleven artists, eight of whom are from the United Kingdom. Is it any wonder that queueing and rain are their media of choice?

The English do not ask much of their weather. Unlike the French, who never met weather that they liked, the English are stoic about the sodden picnic, the blustery boat ride up the Thames, or the muddy outdoor wedding reception. It takes a lot to spoil their fun, as Starbucks acknowledged when it advertised its first stores in England with images of people wearing summer clothes and drinking iced coffees in a downpour. The English will persist in enjoying their gardens and beaches during suboptimal weather in the same way that Manhattanites will happily swelter while inhaling exhaust fumes and fending off panhandlers at their outdoor cafés. If you visit, do the English a favor and go along with it—don't insult them by complaining. The English feel about their weather like you feel about certain disreputable members of your family. It is okay for them to whinge (complain) about it, but outsiders had better not.

The English have a reputation for spending an inordinate amount of time talking about the weather, and this is justified. You will never go wrong leading with the weather, or picking up someone else's weather-related conversational cue, unless you take it upon yourself to disagree with him. Because—*shhh!*—the weather in England is not really that variable. In Hertford, Hereford, and Hampshire, hurricanes *never* happen. You get some rain, you get some sun; it gets a little warmer and colder throughout the year, and sometimes within the same day. A snowy winter is an anomaly. There isn't much to disagree about, and that is why it's such a good conversation-starter for a habitually reserved people. As Shakespeare wrote (though he let the fool sing it): "the rain it raineth every day."

Rain isn't so bad if you remember to bring your umbrella, or brolly. Not everyone uses this admittedly old-fashioned and upper-middle-class locution, but it's still around and, I think we can all agree, far more charming than most diminutives used by the English (like *brekkie* and *biccie* for *breakfast* and *biscuit*). Umbrellas have been around since 1000 BC, and the technology hasn't changed much in the intervening years. (Though the US Patent Office has four staff members dedicated full-time to assessing new applications from Americans who think they can improve on it.) In my experience, English people are far more likely than Americans to have a brolly on hand when they need it. A sunny day with no rain forecast is no guarantee. It's not pessimism, exactly—just the triumph of experience over hope. Most people have a small wardrobe of umbrellas for all eventualities, so they won't be "caught out": cheap ones to keep under their desks at work, tiny ones that fit in a coat pocket or purse, sturdy ones for country walks, and posh ones to carry to weddings or out to dinner on a wet summer night. There's almost no place you can't buy an umbrella in England, but for those who want the best, the world's first all-umbrella shop, James Smith & Sons, has been serving the public since 1830 at number 53 New Oxford Street.

Brollies are perfect for the rain that rains straight down from the sky, and essential for the occasional freak hailstorm (which usually leads to giddy laughter in the street, even though those little pellets of ice *really sting*). But sometimes it rains sideways, or as an enveloping mist that almost seems to emanate from the ground up. That's when you need the getup best described by A. A. Milne in his poem "Happiness": "Great Big Waterproof Boots . . . a Great Big Waterproof Hat . . . [and] a Great Big Waterproof Mackintosh."

No one does rainwear like the English. Barbour waxed cotton jackets and Burberry trench coats are to be seen everywhere, even in high summer. There is some shame in having a new one, though. The most legit level of wear is somewhere between "rumpled university professor" and "tattered gamekeeper." Continual wet weather makes it surprisingly easy to achieve this aesthetic ideal.

Some Americans like to make fun of the English for dwelling on their monotonous weather, but those who do are missing the point. Weather talk is the universal small talk among the English—perhaps the only acceptable pretense for starting a conversation with a stranger, or a neighbor for that matter. If you don't engage in it, you may be throwing away your best chance at connection. Weather talk can be idle or it can be a gateway to something more, and there's only one way to find out.

Americans like their weather big and dramatic—and their weather obliges with hurricanes, tornadoes, nor'easters, and snowstorms. There is tremendous variation in temperature within most states and from one end of the country to the other. This appeals to Americans' self-dramatizing tendency to believe that weather happens not just *around* them, but *to* them. Some types of storms are even given names. The National Hurricane Center has been naming Atlantic hurricanes since 1953, alphabetically in chronological order: Ana, Bill, Claudette, Danny . . . (Until 1979, hurricanes were given only feminine names, but now the genders alternate.) The lists are recycled every six years and a name within a given list is changed only when a particularly devastating hurricane comes along—at which point its name is "retired." Ironically, it is often the mildest-sounding storms that wreak the most havoc: In the beginning, Hurricane Irene may have sounded like a storm that you could have asked to babysit your kids, or sent to Starbucks to buy you a venti skinny latte, but before the week was out she had the coastline in a chokehold, causing sixty-seven deaths and approximately sixteen billion dollars in damage.

The Weather Channel has recently begun to name winter storms, aiding the fast spread of information via Twitter and other social media. Storm-name hashtags were popular already. Americans jump at the chance to name a big snowstorm, and their unofficial, non-Weather-Channel-sanctioned names are mostly derived from the titles of Hollywood movies: "Snowmageddon," "Snowpocalypse," and even "Kaisersnoze" after the quietly diabolical character played by Kevin Spacey in *The Usual Suspects*. American weather can feature such oddities as "thundersnow," which is just what it sounds like. It isn't hard to see how some goofball hit upon the concept for the movie *Sharknado*: "When a freak hurricane swamps Los Angeles, nature's deadliest killer rules sea, land, and air as thousands of sharks terrorize the waterlogged populace!" It almost sounds plausible.

Americans talk about extreme weather with a *Where were you when?* nostalgia they otherwise reserve for political assassinations. They watch the Weather Channel obsessively, and not just for local news. There's always a state of emergency being declared somewhere. Storm-chaser shows and storm-chaser tours, disaster tourism—all were invented by Americans. Deep down, we all love it when "regularly scheduled programming" is interrupted, as long as the storm isn't bearing down on us personally. As the atmospheric pressure drops, spirits rise.

The exception to this weather-induced excitability is quite important, though: It is okay to get worked up about weather that is unusual, or happening elsewhere in America, but you must not react too strongly to weather that is considered normal for your area. There are places where extreme weather is just business as usual. In Minnesota, several feet of snow can fall within a few hours—in April—and go unmentioned, even by people with flights to catch. A couple of Minnesotans I know are happy to run outside whether it's 85 degrees or –34 degrees Fahrenheit—this, they cheerfully describe as a "nice broad range" of temperatures that would surprise no one in their neck of the woods. A Floridian friend wouldn't be caught dead running when the temperature dips below 30—but then again, she'd consider it pathetic to complain about the humidity where she lives (which is like being hit in the face with a wet sponge every time you walk outside).

Both the English and Americans look on bad weather as a test for their elected officials' response in a crisis. Woe betide if they are found wanting—the schadenfreude alone could kill, but in the worst of these failures, the damage is shocking and nothing to laugh at. On the one hand, you have Georgia governor Nathan Deal's public apology for the state's poor preparation after a several-inch snowfall in January 2014 caused residents to abandon their cars on highways and required intervention from the National Guard—an event the locals of "Atlantarctica" genteelly dubbed "ClusterFlake." On the other hand, there's the response of New Orleans mayor Ray Nagin in the aftermath of Hurricane Katrina, which left 80 percent of his city underwater and killed more than 1,800 people, many by drowning. Perhaps frustrated by the way everyone kept looking to *him* for answers, Nagin decided to blame the man upstairs: "Surely God is mad at America. He's sending hurricane after hurricane after hurricane."

English politicians don't have it any easier. Excessive rain in England leads to terrible floods in the countryside every few years, with homes and businesses, livestock and livelihoods at risk. Whenever this happens, London-dwelling politicians of all parties rush out in their Land Rovers to comfort the afflicted, only to be derided for "wellie tourism." Articles appear in the local and national papers with headlines like "Wallies in Wellies: Flood Victims Face a New Deluge of Politicians." (*Wally* is slang for a useless or ineffectual person.) Princes Harry and William earned praise during the latest inundation for showing up with the military to help with sandbagging, but it was too little, too late. There are few elements more implacable, destructive, and downright terrifying than water. When you've seen what a bit more rain than usual can do, the English fascination with weather stops seeming like a punch line. And a room where rain bends to human will starts looking pretty brilliant, even from the back of a daylong queue.

Bespoke

In which a venerable old word is seized upon by
vulgarians—but not Americans.

Not long ago, a highly civilized exchange took place on the Internet. A tailor (English) and a haberdasher (American) found themselves in wholehearted agreement on the meaning of a word that both felt had become degraded: *bespoke*. Thomas Mahon had just clarified the meaning for readers of his blog, "English Cut": "A lot of people use the terms 'bespoke' and 'made-to-measure' interchangeably. They are mistaken. 'Bespoke' . . . dates from the 17th century, when tailors held full lengths of cloth in their premises. When a customer chose a length of material, it was said to have 'been spoken for.' Hence, a tailor who makes your clothes individually, to your specific personal requirements, is called 'bespoke.' . . . ['Made-to-measure'] uses a basic, pre-existing template pattern, which is then adjusted to roughly your individual measurements." Bespoke tailoring has been going on in England—specifically on Savile Row—for a couple of centuries. In America, not so much. Mr. Jeff Collins, professional haberdasher, responded in the comments: "Here in the United States of America, it is very difficult to find someone who does what you do. Most clothing is made to measure, like most of what I provide for my clients, and it bothers me when others in my profession claim to make a 'bespoke' suit. They use the term too loosely. There is something exclusive and regal about wearing a bespoke suit."

A Savile Row bespoke suit takes about one hundred hours to make and, depending on the materials used, costs between £3,000 and £10,000. Everything, from the pattern to the buttonholes, is handmade, and the customer usually has four fittings to ensure perfection. *Bespoke* is not a word that has historically had relevance to 99.999 percent of English people. Kings, rock stars, and oligarchs are among the lucky few who are willing and able to pay for the privilege of so much choice today. But then, the rich (no matter their nationality) have always taken a lot of choices for granted.

The word *bespoke* is virtually unknown in America, which is astonishing because you would think that the American advertising industry would love to get its grubby mitts on a classy word like that. But just because the word is seldom heard and the typical American man wears mostly khakis or jeans and sneakers doesn't mean America lacks the concept. "Having it your way" is considered a birthright by Americans, who bring a curatorial zeal to almost everything they do.

Clothing may not be bespoke in America, but want to know what is? Sandwiches. No one behind the deli counter will raise an eyebrow as you order to your eleven exacting specifications. Then, they will make it, fast, with no eye-rolling. Did I mention this is also cheap? When I went back to America, after a long absence, I was a little miffed when my roast (NOT honey roast) turkey, Swiss cheese, spicy mustard, light mayo, pickles, tomatoes, no lettuce, on whole wheat had gone up to $6.50. However, when it arrived it was not only a work of art, but a truly intimidating size.

In England, most of the 11.5 billion sandwiches (pronounced "samwidges") people buy each year are premade and packed in wedge-shaped cardboard boxes with little cellophane windows offering a preview of their gooey or wilted contents. Depending on how fancy your purveyor, that could be anything from cheese and pickle (a somewhat cloying brown relish made from onions) to prawn mayonnaise (shrimp salad) or my personal favorite, chicken and avocado with pine nuts (don't hate). Pret A Manger (the French name lets you know it's middle-class; the absence of the circumflex and grave accent reassures you you're still in England) is one of the most popular sandwich shops, offering about twenty choices of sandwich every day, with seasonal menu changes. A few branches have opened in New York and in Target stores in America, and the chain is gaining a following. This is partly because of diligent market research. Pret caters to American tastes and hasn't assumed that the same offerings would sell in both countries. But novelty has also played a role in their success, and novelty wears off. Eat a prepacked and arbitrarily sized sandwich for lunch every day and you will soon tire of the standard fillings and the cutesy convenience of their little boxes. Lunch at Pret is more expensive than at the local deli. They offer the comforting illusion of choice and the promise that all the sandwiches were "made fresh in this shop today!" ("Made fresh today" is an attribute one would hope to take for granted in a sandwich, but apparently that ship has sailed.)

A friendly warning to Americans: Accepting standardized sandwiches could be the beginning of the end of choice as you know it. It smacks of socialism. Pretty soon, those who want something a bit more personalized will have to do what the English do and resort to "bespoke" sandwich bars, which will either make the thinnest, saddest version of your favorite sandwich ever (trying to compete with Pret on price) or take ages to deliver something gorgeous that will have you pawning your firstborn in no time. And nothing will save you from the amount of eye-rolling you will have to endure if your rigorous quality standards exceed five directives, no matter how politely phrased. Mayo, fine, but "light" mayo? "Bloody 'ell!" you can hear the guy thinking. This is not choice as Americans have come to expect it. Even Burger King lets you have it your way.

It would be unfair to say that a nation ends up with the sandwiches it deserves. But it is fair to say that a nation gets the sandwiches it *demands*. While the premade sandwiches that most English people eat for lunch are quite good (in their sense of *quite*), they represent an acceptance of not getting exactly what you want. You may get something you like, choosing among set options, but you are not invited to start from scratch, to choose your own adventure. Where is England's sense of entitlement?

I'm going to go out on a limb and blame Hitler. During World War II, a typical weekly ration of food in England included about four pieces of bacon, four ounces of margarine, two ounces of butter, one ounce of cheese, a bit of tea, and eight ounces of sugar. Leaving the sugar aside, it would be hard to turn that into a single lunch today. Meat was allocated by price, and other foods like canned goods and grains required points to buy. Rationing went on, to varying degrees, from 1940 until 1954. While Americans were enjoying the postwar boom, the English were making do and mending for nine more *years*.

People who were children during rationing have especially vivid memories of the food they ate. The BBC keeps an archive of first-person stories about the war, and it's full of homely and fascinating details. The relative lack of sweets meant that a carrot on a stick was considered a treat. Bananas, which are wasted in quantity today as they go brown on kitchen counters everywhere, were the stuff of legend. In Auberon Waugh's memoir, *Will This Do?* he tells of a time when every child in Britain was rationed a single banana. He had never tasted one. When his mother arrived home with three bananas, his father, Evelyn, promptly consumed all three, with cream and sugar, in front of his anguished children. Many years later, his son wrote (unconvincingly), "It would be absurd to say that I never forgave him."

Another man who grew up in wartime writes that whether or not he would clean his plate was "not subject to debate." If he did not, he was "admonished for ingratitude and told in no uncertain terms that there was a child somewhere in the world who would be very glad to eat what was in front of me . . . As a consequence, I perfected a sensory art . . . involving first sniffing the food, and then . . . rapidly shoveling up and swallowing the despised comestibles without permitting any portion of them to make contact with my tongue." This generation of plate-cleaners would reach adulthood—and more prosperous times—only to subject their children to the same rule.

Austerity meant that the few pleasures of the table came

from unlikely sources. A woman writes, "One highlight for me was the coming of spam from America. It was an oasis in our desert of mediocrity; an elixir in our sea of austerity. It seems to me that it was meatier, juicier, and much tastier than it is now. (Tricks of memory again, no doubt.) We ate it in sandwiches; we ate it fried with chips; cold with salad; chopped in spam-and-egg pies, until, of course, it ceased to provide the variety we longed for, but I never tired of it." Not for nothing is Monty Python's SPAM skit one of their best known.

People's memories of wartime deprivation are tinged with a palpable sense of pride. The fairness of rationing and the shared fears and challenges brought people together and showed them how tough and resilient they really were. There is genuine nostalgia—even sentimentality—about those years in England now. Enduring a war on home soil instilled a sense of duty and national pride. It also lowered people's expectations and stopped individuals imagining that their desires could, or should, be the center of the universe. This sense of entitlement only began its slow recovery around the 1980s and, funnily enough, that was when Pret A Manger, with its dizzying varieties of sandwiches *made fresh today*, came to be.

The war has many lingering legacies, and one of them is the idea that "you get what you get and you don't get upset." This is often repeated to small children in England. Another axiom is " 'I want' never gets." This is to encourage politeness ("Please may I have . . .") and to quell the unvarnished id that children haven't yet learned to mask with justifications, as adults have. This is a worthy goal, but it is hard to imagine an American parent using the same means to the end. These sentiments are so un-American it is not even funny. Give it another generation and they probably won't be very English, either. Blame the marketers.

The shops in England that offer the most choice today are actually borrowing the word *bespoke* from Savile Row: *bespoke* cakes, *bespoke* sandwiches, *bespoke* coffees. Everything is spoken for now. The dumbing down of the concept of *bespoke* in its native country would make Mr. Collins, haberdasher, of the USA, want to stick a needle in his eye. It may sound a bit silly, but it represents a level of choice that is actually new for England. It's about time. Americans' expectation of choice can come across as childish, selfish, and fickle to the English. And it is true that the more often you get what you demand, the more likely it is that you will start to believe it's because you deserve it—an unattractive attitude at any age. But consider: If Elvis had been English, we would not have the fried peanut butter, banana, and bacon sandwich. America brought us the Dagwood, the Philly cheesesteak, and the club sandwich—apparently a favorite of the Duke of Windsor and his wife, Wallis Simpson, who knew a little something about the pros and cons of choosing your own adventure. Because as Americans say, if you don't ask, you don't get. But also: Be careful what you wish for.

Fortnight

In which we unpack the reasons why the English take more—and longer—vacations than Americans.

C. S. Lewis wrote that "the future is something which everyone reaches at the rate of 60 minutes an hour, whatever he does, whoever he is." For all their differences, Americans and the English have very similar attitudes toward time. Both cultures value punctuality and hard work and live by the clock. They share a sense of time as a resource that can be saved, spent, or wasted, though perhaps only an American would express the opinion, in earnest, that "time is money." They do have subtly different ways of expressing the passage of time, but these are never sources of lasting confusion. The English write their dates starting with the day first, followed by the month and then the year. Americans start with the month. The English use a twenty-four-hour clock, in which

4:30 P.M. is expressed as "16.30" whenever precision is called for, such as scheduling (pronounced *sheduling*) meetings or talking about train or flight times. With the exception of their military, Americans go by a twelve-hour clock. Americans say "four thirty" or "half past four." The English do, too, but they also might say "half four." The English have a special word, *fortnight*, that means two weeks. Americans just say *two weeks*.

Two weeks—*one bloody fortnight*—is the amount of time the English are appalled to hear that Americans "only" have for *holiday* (vacation) each year. This is perhaps the one point of true divergence when it comes to English and American attitudes toward time. The English get—and take—at least twenty days of vacation, plus public holidays (called *bank holidays*), amounting to a full month of paid vacation each year. Twenty days is the minimum allowed under European Union rules, and England is surrounded by countries where people take even more vacation than the English do. The French get about nine weeks, and even the Germans have eight, which does not seem like something Angela Merkel would have signed off on. Paid vacation is therefore seen as a human right, not a privilege, and the English feel fully entitled to take advantage of it. This results in genuinely slow times of year when few people are at their desks. About 60 percent of UK residents take their main vacations (of at least a fortnight) in July and August, during the school holidays, and the country comes to a virtual standstill during the week between Christmas and New Year's Day. This is one of the single most civilized aspects of life in one of the most civilized countries in the world.

In stark contrast, the United States is the only advanced economy that does not guarantee workers any paid vacation, and

one of only a few rich countries (including Japan) that doesn't require employers to provide any paid holidays. Although 77 percent of US companies do offer paid vacations and holidays, a
quarter of Americans get none at all. The typical worker gets just
ten days per year, along with six public holidays—and this only
after being employed by the same company for at least a year.

Americans who are lucky enough to be entitled to paid vacation very often leave this perk on the table. According to a recent
study by the staffing firm Adecco USA, 75 percent of workers
will not have taken all of their vacation days by November. Although it is tempting to say that this is because of their strong
Puritan work ethic, it is more likely because they are under pressure not to take time off, or are saving up for a few days with
family at Christmas, since at most American companies it's
business as usual on December 26, a day the English know as a
public holiday called Boxing Day. Americans who manage to go
on vacation rarely truly disconnect, and some check in with the
office daily. Otherwise, they risk being seen as slackers, or resented by their peers. It is telling that the Adecco study showed
that 65 percent of respondents said they would like to have two
to three additional weeks of vacation time, even though most of
them weren't using the time they already had.

It is not unusual for the English to take a vacation as long as
a fortnight a couple of times each year, and their close proximity
to other countries in Europe means it is common for them to
travel abroad, usually in search of the sun that's in short supply
in their own country. Most head for the south of France, Spain,
and Portugal. Here I feel compelled to note that, although the
English make fun of Americans for saying French words with an
ersatz accent—fill-ay, buff-ay—and they will aggressively mis-

pronounce these words—*fill-ET*, *buffy*—when they go on holiday in Spain, the same people have no compunction about putting on a Spanish accent to tell you they have been to "Eyebeetha" or "Marbayah." Ibiza and Marbella are known for their glamorous clubs and chilled-out beaches—the destinations of the fit and the tan-aspiring. Some sunny and cheap destinations are more popular with English pensioners (retirees)—like the Algarve region of Portugal, which my friend Catherine has dubbed the "Algrave." One almost feels sorry for these refugee retirees, forced in their desperation for a bit of reliable weather to colonize unsuspecting corners of southern Europe, where they flock together, importing all of their own food and neglecting to learn Portuguese or Spanish. All that this proves is that every country really needs—no, deserves—its very own Boca Raton.

Around 80 percent of UK citizens have passports, and other countries in Europe account for most of their trips abroad. Their most popular destinations outside Europe are very adventurous by American standards: Cyprus, Egypt, North Africa, Goa, and Gambia—closely followed by Florida. Although the tendency of the English to travel on package holidays to all-inclusive resorts means that they cannot lay claim to the title of world's most intrepid travelers, they make it farther afield than most Americans. They do it younger, too, thanks to the somewhat recent tradition—at least among better-off students—of taking a gap year, or twelve-month holiday, before starting university. This is made possible in part by cheaper university fees, which mean that English students can expect to graduate with less debt than Americans. Also, the English can use their EU passports to work abroad, so they don't have to sponge off their parents, though many do anyway.

A 2013 Cheapflights.com survey showed that 85 percent of Americans prefer to return to places that they know rather than take a gamble on a new destination. This may be why New York, Florida, California, Nevada, and Hawaii account for 98 percent of American travel. William D. Chalmers, author of *America's Vacation Deficit Disorder*, laments the days when American families used to light out for the territory in their cars, and quotes Charles Kuralt's depressing observation that "Thanks to the Interstate Highway System, it is now possible to travel across the country from coast to coast without seeing anything." Chalmers has estimated that fewer than 5 percent of Americans travel overseas, even though the latest State Department statistics indicate that 46 percent have passports—a higher percentage than ever before.

America is a wonderful and richly varied country in which to travel—just ask any of the four million UK residents who vacationed there last year. It is also an expensive, difficult, and time-consuming country to get around (and leave). Trains are slow and antiquated. Gas prices may be famously low by comparison to most other countries, but the distances one must cover by car are staggering. When I was a child, living in south Florida, it took my family a minimum of eight hours to get to Disney World, in the middle of the state, and another five to get to the state line.

Is it any wonder that Disney World and visits to Grandma in Savannah were our typical vacations? We rarely flew as a family, and we only knew three or four families who ever made it to Europe—usually to visit relatives. Epcot's World Showcase, with its eleven ersatz "countries"—Mexico, Norway, China, Germany, Italy, Japan, Morocco, France, the United Kingdom, Canada, and (weirdly) the good old USA—was as close as I got to leaving America before the age of nineteen, and I was absolutely enthralled by it: the damp, drainlike smells of the Mexican and Norwegian pavilions (which must have emanated from their water features), the pastries of "France" mixing queasily with the sushi from "Japan" as we toddled off to Future World.

In the past few decades, air travel has become cheaper and more accessible in America and England, but no more pleasant. Stories of indignities endured by low-cost airline passengers abound, but it is hard to imagine a worse experience than that provided by Ryanair, one of Europe's most popular discount airlines. Up until the moment of takeoff, fliers are nickel-and-dimed with charges for printing boarding passes, checking bags, bringing carry-ons, and selecting seats. Between takeoff and landing, surly staff hector them with a variety of small-time sales pitches—newspapers, drinks, snacks, even scratch-off lottery tickets. ("Now is the time on Ryanair when we poke you in the eye with a sharp stick. Goggles, ten euro!") If you play by their Byzantine rules, though, the flights are dirt cheap. The English have learned to live with this in order to stretch their travel budgets—sometimes, it pays to be willing to leave in the middle of the night or fly to out-of-the-way regional airports (a voluntary simulation of the jet lag they might otherwise miss out on by traveling within Europe). Americans have had a harder time coming to terms with the compromises of budget fares. They can't seem to get over their outrage at getting exactly what they've paid for.

The British pound is so strong that for the English, many destinations are cheaper than a week at home. Especially America. For a while you could not swing a cat in a Florida airport without hitting an English tourist with an empty suitcase, ready to fill up with tax-free shopping. Hotel corridors are littered with their discarded shopping bags and boxes. Every London taxi driver has seemingly been able to treat his family to a week on Miami Beach. For Americans, Europe is comparatively expensive. Most items cost in pounds or euros what they would in dollars at home—so shopping isn't very affordable. One is more likely to find Americans at the museums, some of which are generously free in England, whereas a visit to the Museum of Modern Art in New York will set you back twenty-five dollars. They also favor cultural sites for the chance to marvel at architecture that predates any in America by hundreds of years.

The English like to vacation in their own country, and they do visit historic houses and places like Stonehenge and Stratford-upon-Avon. But the twee quaintness of much of it is old hat to them. Many live in houses that bring them into daily contact with the way people lived in ye olden times. For example, a drafty bathroom is tacked onto the back of a house because bathrooms did not exist when it was built. Closets are few and far between. The English are in touch with their history in quotidian ways that Americans aren't, but it isn't necessarily by choice. English homes can be quite uncomfortable—even the newer ones, as English homes are shrinking in size. The Royal Institution of British Architects reports that in 1920, average homes usually measured 1,647 square feet and had four bedrooms, while today's equivalent has three bedrooms and is 925 square feet. The average one-bedroom flat is now the same size as a London Underground carriage.

American homes are generally much larger. In 2011, the average new home was 2,480 square feet, up eighty-eight square feet from the previous year. Anxiety about paying for these ever-larger and more comfortable homes might be one factor keeping Americans on their toes at work, and stopping them from taking their much-needed vacations. But if Americans could be said to be more at ease at home, the English are almost certainly more at ease in the world.

Clever

In which we detect a common thread of anti-intellectualism running through both countries.

I'm not the smartest fellow in the world, but I can sure pick smart colleagues."

"It's not that I'm so smart, it's just that I stay with problems longer."

If you ask an American whether it's good to be smart, he would likely say yes. But ask an American if he himself is smart, and you're likely to get a deflection. The two examples above came from Franklin D. Roosevelt and Albert Einstein, who was an American by immigration rather than by birth and was so smart that his name is synonymous with *genius*, though Americans are far more likely to use it as an ironic insult than a compliment. "Nice one, Einstein!" has followed many a mistake. But while Roosevelt may have been buttering up his cabinet and Einstein encouraging the masses to try harder, there's no doubt that Americans have an ambivalent relationship with the word *smart*. Listen to the way they use it, and you might question whether they think being smart is really such a good thing after all:

> "I've had it with your smart-ass comments."

> "No one likes a smart aleck."

> "Don't get smart with me!"

In America, it's perfectly fine to be a show-off if you are a talented athlete, or musician, or entrepreneur, but it's not cool to be too intellectual. The brightest kids in school are rarely the most liked or popular, and this can last into adulthood if they don't figure out where braininess is welcome and where it isn't.

No one wants smart people lording it over them. It's why people who go to top universities won't mention them by name in mixed company. "I went to college in Boston" is code for "I went to Harvard, but please like me anyway." Americans don't like elitism—and they associate intellectualism with elitism. This has been one of Barack Obama's recurring challenges as president. His critics look for every opportunity to prove he is, as *The New York Times* reported, "a Harvard-educated millionaire elitist who is sure that he knows best and thinks that those who disagree just aren't in their right minds. Never mind that Mr. Obama was raised in less exalted circumstances by a single mother who he said once needed food stamps. Or that although he went to private school, he took years to pay off his college loans. Something about Mr. Obama's cerebral confidence has made him into a symbol of something he never used to be." The *Onion* has repeatedly mined this rich vein of humor, declaring, "Overjoyed civil rights leaders" say that Barack Obama is "redefining who can be smeared as condescending eggheads" now that Americans are "able to look past Obama's skin color to see the Harvard-educated smart-ass underneath." By contrast, a lot of Americans considered President George W. Bush kind of dumb—he was known for his malapropisms and loved to brag about having been a "C" student—but they never accused him of being an elitist, even though he graduated from Andover, Yale, and Harvard and came from one of America's most successful political dynasties. Which likely shows how not-dumb he really is.

The English have a word for a person with that kind of intelligence—*clever*—and it's not usually a compliment. A common English expression is "too clever by half," which implies arrogance and overconfidence in one's intelligence—the kind of display that others find annoying or overbearing. In the popular children's television program *Peppa Pig*, in which anthropomorphic mammals of many kinds live in the same town (and are all, bizarrely, the same size—from pigs to rabbits and cats, dogs, and even zebras), Edmond, the youngest son in the Elephant family, goes around correcting museum guides' patter and knows all there is to know about dinosaurs, among other things. Whenever he gives one of his irritating know-it-all speeches, he makes a little trumpeting noise and says, "I'm a Clever Clogs!" *Clever Clogs* is a slightly pejorative name for a person of above-average intelligence and below-average modesty. This joke goes down well in a country where "blowing one's own trumpet" is simply not done. There might even be a spot of childhood indoctrination going on.

There are two other words in English English that have sim-

ilar meanings: *boffin* and *anorak*. An *anorak* is someone (usually male) with an obsessive interest in a niche subject (so
named for the none-too-fashionable windbreakers they often
wear—think Cliff Clavin in *Cheers*). *Boffin* is a slightly more af-
fectionate term, which originated during World War II as a
name for the technical experts, engineers, and codebreakers
who helped win the war. Today it is used, as Robert Hutton notes
in his book *Romps, Tots and Boffins*, primarily in news headlines about "anyone with a job at a university, a science GCSE
[General Certificate of Secondary Education] or a lab coat."

In England, like America, playing up your intelligence is
just plain bad manners—not because it's uncool to be bright, or
because it's considered elitist, but because it's showing off, and
as Sarah Lyall asserts in her book, *A Field Guide to the British*,
"boasting . . . makes you seem aggressive, ambitious, self-
regarding, puffed up—verging on American. The evils of those
things are ingrained in them at school, where they are discour-
aged from saying they are better than anyone else, even when
they are." Even Oscar Wilde, one of the biggest show-offs the
British Isles ever produced, knew this. He made valiant attempts at self-deprecation, but never really carried it off, once
saying, "I am so clever that sometimes I don't understand a single word of what I am saying."

Elitism doesn't sit much easier with the English than it does
with Americans, but there is less ambiguity about who can be
justly accused of it. Like President Obama, Prime Minister
David Cameron often has to defend himself against charges of
elitism, but he comes from a genuinely posh background and
has been criticized for installing many of his Old Etonian chums
in key advisory roles and being unprepared to speak for "ordi-

nary" voters. It's his bad luck to have been so expensively educated, because if he were choosing to hire childhood friends from the state comprehensive, it would make for better publicity. (An English "state school" is the equivalent of an American "public school," while in England some elite private schools are called "public.") Interestingly, Cameron and his wife, Samantha, have declared their intention to send their daughter to a state secondary school, where she can have a "normal" education. Cameron will be the first Conservative prime minister to send a child to a state school while in office.

More visible hierarchies and class distinctions mean that the English can be much more specific and articulate about these tensions and resentments than Americans, and they tend to use humor to defuse them. For example, one reason cleverness has acquired a bad name in England is that middle-class parents are forever harping on about how "bright" their own children are—often by way of excuse for their terrible behavior. Jeremy Hardy imitated a middle-class father in a hilarious rant on BBC Radio 4: "Hermione's so *bright*, and that's why she misbehaves, I think. She's so much *brighter* than the other children, and that's why she sets fire to them, I think." There has long been a conviction among the English that clever people are, well, not very *nice*. To be candid, not everyone minds—the English find it more acceptable than Americans to be cruel in the service of wit—but a poem by Dame Elizabeth Wordsworth captures the conflict:

> If all the good people were clever,
> And all clever people were good,
> The world would be nicer than ever
> We thought that it possibly could.

> But somehow 'tis seldom or never
> The two hit it off as they should,
> The good are so harsh to the clever,
> The clever, so rude to the good!

Dame Elizabeth was the great-niece of the poet William Wordsworth and the principal of Lady Margaret Hall, one of the Oxford colleges, from 1879–1909, when she founded St Hugh's Hall to educate poor female undergraduates. This was later established as St Hugh's College, which is today the largest of the thirty-eight colleges in Oxford University. So it would seem she was one of those rare birds, clever as well as good. The last stanza of her poem gives us all reason to hope that clever doesn't always have to be a pejorative—if we're smart about it.

> So friends, let it be our endeavour
> To make each by each understood;
> For few can be good, like the clever,
> Or clever, so well as the good.

Ginger

In which ancient conflicts and prejudices continue to make life difficult for English redheads.

once read an amusing article about "beauty lag" that compared women's grooming habits in London, New York, and Los Angeles. The farther west, apparently, the more lacquered and "done" a woman is expected to look. (London: fresh haircut, clean fingernails. New York: blowout, manicure. Los Angeles: all of the above plus highlights, pedicure, and fake bake.) My own experience bears this out. Yet standards of beauty don't differ much from one side of the Atlantic to the other, with one exception.

A redhead in America will be considered enviable and special, if occasionally subjected to dunderheaded stereotypes about her supposed volatility or fiery temper. Children in the schoolyard will tease anyone for what makes him different, and red hair is no exception. But American associations with red hair include Charles Schulz's little red-haired girl—the object of Charlie Brown's affection in the *Peanuts* comics. She was based on an unrequited love of Schulz's, and such was his reverence for the character that he never drew her, preferring to let her live in readers' imaginations. In America, people with naturally red hair (who represent just 2 percent of the population) are widely imitated. Actresses like Christina Hendricks and Emma Stone have inspired a rush to hairdressers.

In England, by contrast, redheads are taunted and ridiculed for life, even subjected to random acts of violence. They are known as "ginger," which is not merely descriptive but can be a term of abuse. American actress Jessica Chastain told *GQ* that while on location in Thailand, "I'd be walking down the street and people—British people—would stop the car and scream, 'ginger!' at me." English model Lily Cole has also been bullied for her hair color. She told the *Mail on Sunday*: "I remember feeling very insecure. When I'd meet people, I would think they wouldn't like me—that was an actual thought process—because I'm a redhead. It's absolutely absurd."

The dangers of "gingerism" go beyond bullying. Recent reports include a stabbing, a family forced to move twice after their children were teased mercilessly, a woman who won a sexual harassment suit after being targeted for her red hair, and a boy who committed suicide after being intimidated by other teens. These incidents prompted Nelson Jones in the *New Statesman* to ask, "Should ginger-bashing be considered a hate crime?" He argued, "If the concept has any meaning, it should apply irrespective of the personal characteristic, innate or adopted, cultural or sartorial, that inspires the hate." The prejudice against this coloring has been likened to racism, and not only in jest, though one of the funnier examples is Australian (redhead) comic Tim Minchin's song "Prejudice," in which he sings of "a word with a terrible history . . . a couple of *G*s, an *R* and an *E*, an *I* and an *N*." His American audiences roar with relieved laughter when the word turns out to be *ginger*. Americans cannot afford to be smug about this, and they know it. Any week of the year, the national news carries evidence that England holds no monopoly on hate, or its related crimes. Yet *ginger* is seldom used, and carries little to no emotional freight, in the United States.

In order to understand this cultural difference, you have to look to a historical antagonism between the English and the Scots and Irish—places with disproportionately high percentages of redheads. The Anglo-Irish War freed the Irish from English rule less than one hundred years ago, and the history of oppression by the English and insurrection by the Irish assured an uneasy peace. Prejudice against the Irish also has a virulent past in America. It arrived with the first settlers from England, and intensified with anxiety over Irish immigration to the United States after the potato famine. As late as the 1800s, Irish-Americans were being compared to apes. Negative stereotypes of them as violent and hard-drinking persisted for much longer.

While many Scots are proud to be part of the United Kingdom, just last year a vocal group—headed by then–first minister Alex Salmond—campaigned for Scotland to end its 307-year union with the UK. On the day of the referendum, voter turnout was higher than in any UK election since 1918, the first time all adults were given the right to vote. Forty-five percent voted "yes" to Scottish independence.

The conflicts between the English and the Irish and Scots may be mostly bloodless now, but they are not forgotten. What is largely forgotten is the context for the English bias against "gingers." This may be one reason that ginger jokes are considered acceptable in a way that racist jokes about nonwhites would never be. Teasing redheads has become disassociated from anti-Irish or anti-Scot feeling, which is a step in the right direction. But the teasing itself—and the random violence—continues.

Redheads in England have started ginger-positive websites and groups, which seek to take back the term. Bloggers and parenting magazines give advice on raising redheads. A mother-daughter team started to offer support and products. Most are keen to let you know that they do not go in for special pleading—they just want to live in peace. As redhead Ally Fogg wrote in *The Guardian*, "I'm pretty sure I have never been denied a job or the lease on a flat . . . I haven't been stopped and searched by police . . . or casually assumed to be a threat, a criminal or a terrorist . . . Nobody wishes to bar me from marrying my partner because she has (peculiarly, I will be the first to admit) fallen in love with a ginger."

Gingerism may not be tantamount to racism, but I think it's telling that Fogg couldn't resist putting a ginger joke into this otherwise serious editorial. In England, pain is most often exorcised through humor. A recurring sketch on the *Catherine Tate Show* had comedian Tate (a redhead) portraying a character named Sandra Kemp, who goes under police protection to "Russet Lodge," a safe house for gingers who've been victimized. In a later sketch, Kemp starts a campaign group called "Gingers For Justice," taking a stand against the public, who have ostracized gingers from society.

Even being fourth in line to the throne doesn't exempt an English redhead from ridicule. Prince William once mocked his brother during an interview, saying that he's a "ginger . . . but he's a good-looking ginger so it's all right." Will it ever end? Unfortunately, neither England nor America can claim that prejudice—racial or otherwise—is a relic of the past. Maybe we ought to give the last word to a fictional Canadian, Anne of Green Gables, who said, "People who haven't red hair don't know what trouble is."

Dude

In which a word typifying American ease is revealed to have had more urbane origins.

Americans are divided over whether they love or hate what they perceive to be the superior refinement—or the finicky preciousness—of the English. Those who *are* attracted to all things English usually cite the "British accent" as one of the reasons for their Anglophilia. The accent they are thinking of is the one they associate with the BBC and costume dramas, like *Downton Abbey*. This clipped and carefully enunciated accent is known as *received pronunciation* (RP), and it is the English corollary of America's General American accent, otherwise known as "newscaster English."

Any American or English person knows that his country's "ideal" accent is not the norm. Even the BBC has stopped insisting on RP. Charlotte Green, once voted the "most attractive female voice on national radio," says her diction means that she is now an outcast at the BBC; she took voluntary redundancy from her job as a newsreader in 2013, saying, "Received pronunciation, or accent-less accent, is on the wane. The BBC's days of employing people who sound like me are more or less over." Each country contains a hodgepodge of regional accents that may be hard for an outsider to tell apart. Yet it's fair to say that the rhythm and tone of all English accents (maybe even all British accents) sound more like one another, to the American ear, than they sound like his own—which is why he lumps them together. You wouldn't expect an English person to be able to tell a Pennsylvania accent from a Baltimore one. The English are just as apt to generalize about "the American accent" as Americans are to generalize about British accents. Interestingly, they associate an American accent with success in business. Khalid Aziz, a communications specialist, surveyed British business directors and found that 47 percent of them considered executives with American accents more successful than their own countrymen.

Americans think that all English people sound posh, and they won't let the English forget it. Those who spend a lot of time in America, especially British expats, aren't thrilled about the constant compliments they get about their accents, and some find them intrusive. There are more than sixty-six thousand members of a Facebook page called "I hate the way Americans think us English people all speak dead posh." (*Dead* can be used in English English to mean "completely," as it is here.)

In England, accent is a strong indicator of one's place in the class hierarchy. Many people grow up feeling self-conscious of what their accents reveal about them, whether they are posh or not, and compliments can make them feel a bit uncomfortable.

Americans, imagine you were driving a Honda Civic and people kept praising it as if it were a Rolls-Royce. It's no wonder the English sometimes wrinkle their noses. American flattery comes too easily for the naturally skeptical English to respect. And here is the truth: The average English person is no more polished or refined than the average American. The impression of refinement is often nothing more than distance, plus unfamiliarity.

That doesn't mean that English expats are annoyed by the perks that come with some Americans' misapprehension. They are happy for people to assume they are intelligent, sophisticated, and authoritative, and for members of the opposite sex to swoon over them. Americans sometimes have occasion to question the qualities they have ascribed to such people. Journalist Vicky Ward recently reported in the *Financial Times* that when the architect Norman Foster, having taken four years to produce his plans for a renovation of the New York Public Library's main branch on Forty-Second Street, unveiled a design that critic Michael Kimmelman described as having "the elegance of a suburban mall," a rival architect confided "that some trustees had begun to feel, too late, that they had been seduced by Lord Foster's 'British accent.'"

The English are constantly exposed to a variety of American accents and vocabulary through television and movies. Americans' less-enunciated accents, and tendency to speak louder than the English are used to, make them sound brash, confident, and a little sloppy. American slang contributes to this impression, cutting across socioeconomic and gender lines far more than English slang, which is stratified. For example, to the English middle and upper classes, something they like will be "brilliant," and if they agree with something you say, they may do so by saying

"Quite." A working-class person from London or Essex, seeking agreement, will use the question tag "innit" at the end of a sentence, in the same way an American might say "amIright?" It is harder to tell Americans' social class from the words they use, and as a result Americans of all classes can sound similarly unrefined.

There is no word that typifies this phenomenon more thoroughly than *dude*. *Dude* is a word that—no matter how often they are exposed to it—the English will not adopt. It is one of the most American-sounding words there is. And the story of *dude* is also the story of how American slang can become universal and classless in a way that is hard to imagine happening in England.

Ironically, this aggressively casual word that, in today's American English, might refer to a person of either sex, originated as a way to describe a dandy or a "swell." The *OED* dates it to New York in 1883 as "a name given in ridicule to a man affecting an exaggerated fastidiousness in dress, speech, and deportment, and very particular about what is aesthetically 'good form.'" This later extended to the meaning implied by "dude ranch": "a non-westerner or city-dweller who tours or stays in the west of the U.S., especially one who spends his holidays on a ranch." A dude was an East Coast city slicker who didn't fit in on the West Coast. But it only took about thirty years for the word to shed these pejorative implications and become, primarily through Black English vernacular, a generally approving term for a man, "a guy."

By the 1960s and '70s, *dude* had cut across racial lines, appearing in movies like *Easy Rider* and songs including David Bowie's "All the Young Dudes," which made a one-hit wonder of the band Mott the Hoople. *Dude* then faded from prominence, perhaps considered a bit of a relic, though it remained in constant use among Californians, stoners, surfers, and suburban Valley girls. Sean Penn's character in the film *Fast Times at Ridgemont High*, Jeff Spicoli, typified this use of *dude*. And who could forget the masterpiece of cinema that was *Dude, Where's My Car?*

The moment that *dude* broke out and acquired its current cultural significance was 1998, when Jeff Bridges played a character known as "the Dude" in the Coen Brothers film *The Big Lebowski*. The Dude hangs around in his bathrobe, drinking White Russians. His habitual occupations? "Oh, the usual. I bowl. Drive around. The occasional acid flashback . . . I'm the Dude. So that's what you call me. You know, that or, uh, His Dudeness, or, uh, Duder, or El Duderino if you're not into the whole brevity thing." The movie became a cult hit and the word itself achieved ubiquity. As Ron Rosenbaum wrote in the *New York Observer*, "Outside of those sad figures who cloister themselves off from the pleasures of pop culture, 'dude' is not just a part of the language—dude is a whole discourse."

Dude today encapsulates a very casual orientation to life. Jeff Bridges's character has spawned a book, *The Dude and the Zen Master*, a collaboration between Bridges and Buddhist teacher Bernie Glassman; *The Dudespaper: A Lifestyle Magazine for the Deeply Casual*; and even a religion, Dudeism—"a belief system that teaches us that the universe wants us to take it easy" since "getting all worked up over nothing goes profoundly against the laws of nature, psychology, sociology, bowling and several tropical countries." This is a nice antidote to the hard-driving, ambitious side of American culture: If you get tired of working hard and playing hard, it promises, ultimately it is possible to just "abide" like the Dude.

As Rosenbaum points out, the word *dude* has also become "a way of bringing a conscious unsophistication—an ironical unsophistication, an unsophistication in quotation marks, a sophisticated unsophistication—to an appreciation of popular culture." In my experience, friends of non-American nationality (English, German, French) use *dude* almost exclusively in this way—poking gentle fun at Americans, while taking advantage of the utility of the word. But I think that most Americans who say it aren't being ironic at all. Some of them are aware that this makes them sound unsophisticated, and seek to break their dependence on *dude*.

On the website IsItNormal.com, a young woman wrote in to say she felt she overused the word: "i can't help it. i say it to my mom. i say it to inanimate objects. i call my boyfriend dude instead of babe or love or even his real name. i've even had somebody yell DUUUUDE in the hallway and turned around on cue. is this normal?" [*sic*] She got a range of responses, many of which suggested she was not alone in her Tourette's-like repetition of *dude*. One person wrote, "If u really need to stop, example for a job?, just use an elastic around your wrist and snap it everytime and make sure it hurts that way saying it = pain to your brain, it will catch on overtime." [*sic*] Someone else (employing another near-universal American slang word) wrote: "im 25 and still have this problem it sucks. Like totally dude, we need to let that word die." And another said, "OMG DUDE SAMEZZZZ." [*sic*—no, really!] Has American addiction to *dude* reached the point where we need a twelve-step program? (Dude, that sounds way too ambitious.)

It's no wonder Americans hear intelligence and refinement in English voices: It is as much about the words they are *not* using as the ones they use. But in the end I think the most authentic thing to do—no matter what your country of origin—is to own and celebrate your native accent and vocabulary. In other words, chill out, dude. It's okay to sound, like, totally American.

Partner

In which an expat finds that her frustration with English reserve is not always justified.

Shortly after moving to London from New York, I began keeping notes about signs, customs, and words that seemed strange to me. I wanted to keep track of first impressions that, within months, would be difficult to recall. Luckily, no one was keeping track of the strange first impressions I myself was making. Some of my early misunderstandings had an audience of one—my husband, Tom.

Over dinner, soon after beginning work in the London offices of the same companies we'd worked for in New York, we were discussing some of the differences between our New York and London colleagues. In New York, people would send their juniors out for coffee (the more complicated the order, the better) to put them in their place. In London, there was a lot of nonhierarchical tea-fetching from a communal kitchen. In New York, people dressed up more to go to work and took little time off. Everyone seemed to work through the weekend. In London, no one talked about how hard they were working and "face time" seemed less important. The New Yorkers had been more status-conscious, but friendlier. The Londoners were edgier and quieter—almost disconcertingly so.

Yet I had managed to glean some details about the lives of my coworkers. For one thing, I told Tom, whereas in New York about 10 percent of my coworkers were gay, in London it must be approaching 60 percent. "Really?" he asked—because even for publishing, that seemed like a lot. "Yes," I said. "Hardly any-one in my office wears a wedding band, and they are always talking about their 'partners' and children. My office must be the most liberal in London." Tom thought I was right that my of-fice was probably the most liberal in London, but he was pretty sure my percentages were off. Because, he explained, in En-gland, unlike in America, *partner* isn't a code word for "same-sex partner." This is a common misapprehension among newly emigrated Americans, and one that we can all laugh about later. A friend of mine spent weeks at her kids' new playgroup before figuring out that most of the other kids did not "have two mommies."

Americans come by this mistake honestly. Although people are getting married older these days, in the United States people tend to assume that most committed relationships are headed for marriage. Regardless of age, the infantilizing *boyfriend* and *girlfriend* apply until the pretentious *fiancé/fiancée* are sup-planted by the cozy *husband* and *wife*. A Pew poll taken in 2010 showed that 61 percent of American adults who have never been married want to be; only 12 percent do not. A poll of high school seniors taken in 2006 showed that 81 percent of them expected to get married, and 90 percent of those expected to stay married to the same person for life. Andrew Cherlin, a sociologist at Johns Hopkins University who studies families and public policy, maintains that in America "you don't see the same pattern of long unmarried relationships you see in Scandinavia, France or Britain . . . In the United States marriage is how we do stable families."

Americans may be big proponents of marriage, but with the third-highest divorce rate in the world, it doesn't mean they are any better at commitment than other nationalities (with the exception of #1, the Maldives, and #2, Belarus). One thing Americans have had a hard time committing to is the idea of universal marriage rights. Until recently, the best a gay or lesbian couple could hope for was *partner*. Opponents of gay marriage have long feared that extending marriage rights to all Americans would undermine the beloved institution. But, as E. J. Dionne Jr. wrote in *The Washington Post*, the opposite seems to be happening, as "steadily increasing numbers of Americans have come to believe that gay people are not social revolutionaries looking to alter the nature of marriage." Rather, they simply want to be "part of an institution that is already open to their straight fellow citizens." In more and more states, this dream is coming true.

In England, by contrast, marriage isn't considered quite so necessary. Since December 2005, it has been possible for same-sex couples to enter into civil partnerships, which confer most of the same rights and responsibilities as marriage, without the name. Heterosexual couples are less likely to marry than their counterparts in America, even when they choose to have children. Fifty-two percent of people in a survey by YouGov said that marrying was "not important, provided that parents were in a committed relationship." Only 27 percent took the view that couples should be married before having children. So in England, it makes sense that the first definition of *partner* in *Macmillan* is "someone who you live with and have a sexual relationship with," whereas in America it is "one of two or more people who own a company and share its profits and losses."

I have noticed that even married people in England will use *partner* rather than *husband* or *wife*. *Macmillan* corroborates this: "In British English, you can say *partner* to refer to a person who is the husband or wife of someone, or to refer to a person who someone is living with and having a sexual relationship with, without being married to them. This avoids mentioning the person's status or sex. In American English, some people only use *partner* about unmarried people, and many others only use it about gay men or women." This note is set apart in a special box under the headline "Words that avoid giving offence." Which kind of nails it. I had been so busy being a nosy American that this elegant subtlety had almost passed me by.

It is always tempting to make generalizations: for example that Americans are so *open* because they will volunteer personal information to relative strangers, and the English are so *reserved* because they won't. But you have to take it case by case. And in the case of *partner*, it's the English who are more open—if not about the details of their private lives, then to the possibilities of other people's. Not to start with an assumption based on the word someone uses—or anything else—is very high-level humanity indeed. The nongendered *partner* leaves something to the imagination—something at which the English excel—so it allows people to choose how much to reveal. Because it really isn't anyone's business whether you and your partner are married, or what gender he or she is.

Of course, not everyone is using *partner* to be inclusive in England any more than Americans are using *husband* and *wife* to be *ex*clusive. Some people aren't consciously choosing, but simply using the word that is most familiar. But many who choose to use *partner* like what it implies: a relationship between equals. As American blogger Jonny Scaramanga explains, "Equality is something I can get behind. I don't have a wife who depends on me. I have an equal. I have a partner."

In England and Wales, same-sex marriages now have the blessing of the Parliament and the queen, and civil partners have the option of converting their unions to marriages. In America, some states have approved same-sex marriage and, with the younger generation of voters overwhelmingly in favor, equal rights to marriage will soon spread. Where will that leave *partner*? Will American gay and lesbian couples, after their long battle for the right to be husbands and wives, choose to use those words to describe themselves? Will English married couples continue to describe themselves as "partners"? And how will anyone know what to call anyone else while we all figure it out? Steven Petrow, author of *Complete Gay & Lesbian Manners*, has a suggestion. We ought to listen "to how a couple introduces or refers to each other . . . Then follow their lead by using their preferred terminology." What a radical idea.

Proper

In which we learn that people—and things—can be proper
without being pretentious.

Sometimes we're so busy looking for what we expect to find that we miss what's actually there. In some ways, Americans and the English are more similar than they think. For example, both nationalities have a preoccupation with authenticity, and they don't like pretension. These are characteristics we would do well to understand—and appreciate—about each other. The English have a way of describing something that is genuine, bona fide, and thoroughly of its kind: *proper.* ("Fursty Ferret is a proper ale.") English people get a kick out of things being "proper." "Proper!" can even stand as a full-fledged compliment. *Proper* can also be used subversively, as an intensifier to a derogatory statement ("Proper rude, isn't she!") or, even more informally, as a synonym for *correctly* ("He never learned to drive proper.")

This definition, while not entirely unknown, is not the primary one in America. If an American hears "a proper cup of tea," he is apt to picture a pinkie-lifting exercise in etiquette—not the strong and hot brew this phrase calls to the English mind. All the most common American uses of the word *proper* are about conforming to convention, being respectable and appropriate, formal and sedate. When Americans call something *proper* they are thinking refined, virtuous, boring. Being proper means likely having to pretend to be something one isn't. Being genuine, or "real," is far more desirable in American society than being proper. What Americans might not realize is that when the English say *proper*, genuine and real is precisely what they mean.

For an example of what *proper* means to the English, look no further than the first meal of the day. A proper breakfast is the full English, otherwise known as the fry-up or the Full Monty. It dates to the Victorian era and, though they may not eat it every day, everyone agrees on what it is: sausage, bacon, fried eggs, fried tomatoes and mushrooms, baked beans, and fried bread. It is usually served with ketchup and HP sauce (a sweet and vinegary "brown sauce," so named because its inventor heard that it was being served in a restaurant at the Houses of Parliament). Now that's proper.

The English Breakfast Society ("Support the Tradition, Share the Love" #FryUp) claims that in the 1950s, half the nation started their day on the full English, and while it especially appealed to those who worked in industrial jobs, the meal is essentially classless—something rare in England, as you may have gathered. There are many regional variations on the porky aspect of the breakfast. In the North there will be black pudding (a sausage made with pigs' blood, pork, and a filler like bread crumbs or rusk), and in Devon and Cornwall, white pudding (similar to black pudding, but without the blood). Each region of England is known for a particular type of sausage. The Cumberland is spiced with pepper; the Gloucester contains Gloucester Old Spot pork and sage; the Yorkshire includes cayenne, nutmeg, white pepper, and mace; and the Lincolnshire sage and thyme. I could go on, but the point is that there is a consensus on what is "proper" when it comes to breakfast in England—even if the full English is widely regarded as hangover food today.

It's not the Industrial Revolution anymore, after all, and few people want to go sit at a desk after eating approximately 1,550 calories—78 percent of an adult woman's requirement for the day, as Jamie Oliver's website helpfully informs us. If you want a lighter version, a health-drink company called Fuel, founded by a former tank commander in the British Army and an extreme-sports enthusiast, offers a liquid fry-up combining the flavors of bacon, sausage, poached egg, fried tomatoes, baked beans, mushrooms, toast, salt and pepper, and brown sauce. It's only 230 calories, and it packs twenty grams of protein (assuming you can keep it down). Apparently scientists had to test five hundred flavor combinations before they hit on this winner—pity the tasters of the 499 rejected shakes. If that doesn't hit the spot, other foods the English eat for breakfast—that don't fall under the heading of the full English but are nevertheless considered "proper"—include kippers (smoked herring), kedgeree (a dish of smoked haddock and hard-boiled eggs with rice, cream, and curry powder, topped with parsley), and kidneys on toast. I never noticed before that these breakfasts are all brought to you by the letter *K*. Luckily, it is no longer true, as W. Somerset Maugham once said, that to eat well in England one must have breakfast three times a day.

There is no consensus in America about what breakfast should be, unless you count the "complete breakfast!" that sugary cereals are said to be "part of" in TV commercials: cereal (Frosted Flakes, Froot Loops, Lucky Charms, Cocoa Puffs), orange juice, toast, eggs, bacon, and fruit, which looks more like a hotel buffet than the average American kitchen table on a weekday morning. America's regional variations are a bit more diverse than England's. A typical Southern breakfast will include grits (ground hominy—dried corn kernels treated with lye). In Pennsylvania they like their scrapple (a loaf made of pork scraps and cornmeal, sliced and fried). In New York, lox and bagels with cream cheese are ubiquitous. In the Southwest, huevos rancheros (eggs with salsa, bell peppers, refried beans, and tortillas) are just the thing for the morning after the night before. Most cities in America, if they don't have a famous local doughnut shop, will at least have Dunkin' Donuts or, even better, Krispy Kreme. Both chains have established a beachhead in England, where there is no native doughnut brand, though jam-filled doughnuts (of the type that originated in Germany) are widely available. Americans share the English love of pork products, and artisanal sausage-making has become a feature of farmers' markets and gourmet groceries, but in most of America if someone asks you your favorite sausage, they are really asking, "links or patties?," referring to the shape of sausage you prefer—small and cylindrical, or burger-shaped.

Still, the classic American breakfast—when regional differences are accounted for—is the diner breakfast. The kind where you order three scrambled eggs and get six. The kind that comes with a "side" of pancakes, as if the eggs and bacon and hash browns weren't going to cut it. Because Americans love a sugary breakfast, and no restaurant seems to get this quite like the American chain diner Denny's. One of their latest menu items is the Peanut Butter Cup Pancake Breakfast, which starts with two chocolate and white chocolate chip buttermilk pancakes, topped with hot fudge and drizzled with "peanut butter sauce." They come with two eggs, hash browns or grits, bacon or sausage, and warm syrup. If this doesn't prove Americans have no sense of propriety when it comes to breakfast, I don't know what does. Perhaps this review of Denny's Apple Pie French Toast, by a blogger named Erin Jackson from San Diego: "The Apple Pie French Toast struck me as a pretty fantastic idea . . . On top of a thick-cut slice of French toast, there's a large spoonful of apple crisp (baked apple slices topped with a brown sugar and butter-heavy crumble), a drizzle of caramel sauce, and some powdered sugar. You get syrup on the side, but . . . if you're going to add anything, make it the last few bites of ice cream from your deep-fried pancake ball sundae."

Americans, perhaps alone among England's international tourists, do not find the full English breakfast a daunting amount of food. Even though, like the English—truth be told—on a typical day at home they either skip breakfast or pick up a muffin or egg sandwich to eat *al desko*. Something everyone can agree is a "proper" breakfast in neither sense of the word.

OK

*In which American earnestness and moral relativism are
shown to be two sides of the same coin.*

The Miss USA pageant has been one of America's apple-
pie events for more than sixty years. True, the television ratings aren't what they used to be, but with
Donald Trump taking over, you can bet that even if the hair
doesn't improve, the numbers will. In 2013, five million jaws
dropped when Miss Utah, Marissa Powell, flamed out in the
Q&A. The question was about women earning less than men.
What did this say about American society?

"I think we can relate this back to education, and how we are
continuing to try to strive to . . ." She hesitated. ". . . figure out
how to create jobs right now. That is the biggest problem and I
think especially the men are, uh, seen as the leaders of this, so

we need to try to figure out how to create education better so that we can solve this problem."

Wags were quick to point out that her home state has the lowest per-pupil spending on education in the nation—quite a distinction. In the aftermath, having lost the pageant to Miss Connecticut, Powell claimed to be grateful for the learning experience: "For myself, just being able to realize that it's OK to be human, it's OK to make mistakes," she said. "Get back up and keep pushing forward and I think that's a lesson I can share with a lot of people which I'm really grateful for." Her response is so American that I would almost argue she deserves the crown.

There was a lot of predictable snark on the next day's talk shows, blogs, and drive-time radio. This quickly gave way to hand-wringing over whether it was "OK" to laugh at Miss Utah's expense, which is even more American. The English would never ask a question like that, because they aren't as earnest as Americans. Americans are *really* earnest—in a way that the English find faintly ridiculous. So while Americans laugh at Miss Utah, they will feel somewhat guilty and wonder if it's OK to do so. They will come to the conclusion that it is OK, as long as it's all in fun, just as Miss Utah will decide that her humiliating gaffe was OK, as long as she (and others!) learned from it.

You could be forgiven for thinking that Americans have a monopoly on *OK*, but of course they don't. *OK* is used worldwide and has analogues in many languages. Many nations have claimed credit for inventing it, and some of their stories are compelling, but I'm sorry to report that the truth is rather prosaic. In his book *OK: The Improbable Story of America's Greatest Word*, Allan Metcalf lays out a convincing case that *OK* first appeared as a lame joke in the *Boston Morning Post* in March 1839. It was a deliberately incorrect abbreviation for "all correct." This used to be common knowledge; over time, *OK* shed its origin story, along with its American accent. It belongs to Globish—not English—now. But, Metcalf argues, *OK* means something more to Americans than it does to the rest of the world. It amounts to a two-letter philosophy of life, expressing Americans' "pragmatism, efficiency, and concern to get things done by hook or by crook."

To this, I would add Americans' essential sincerity. An American and an Englishman might arrive at the same decision, but they do so in a different spirit. The English "muck in"; Americans "help out." The English are resigned; Americans are accepting. The English "mustn't grumble" but Americans "turn lemons into lemonade." Americans are known for "taking it easy." They just say "OK." It is a common American conversational tic to append "OK?" to the end of a sentence. "I'm just going to park here for a minute, OK?" "I'm going to open another bottle of wine, OK?" "I'm just going to send my kids over to your house while I run to the store, OK?" The saying "I'm OK, you're OK" originated as a self-help book title in America and it remains in the culture decades later because it captures something essential about how Americans think and act.

Americans can be moral relativists, but they also want to be liked. They want to do what they want to do, but they feel obligated to justify it to everyone else. Whatever they want, if they want it bad enough, must by definition be "OK." They apply the same logic to everyone else. The Baby Boomers pioneered "if it feels good, do it," but they could accomplish only so much before the Internet. The current generation—of which Miss Utah is one—are raising self-justification to a high art. In their song "It's OK in the USA," the band Jesus H. Christ and the Four Hornsmen of the Apocalypse sing, "It's OK to be fat. It's OK to be loud / OK to be dumb. It's OK to be proud / And if you think your cat's a gourmet, it's OK." That about covers it.

Americans are believers—not just in a religious sense but in the sense of going wholeheartedly down the path they have chosen. This is not always the right path. A high tolerance for mavericks and overconfidence goes with the territory. True genius erupts from this ethos—Benjamin Franklin, Steve Jobs, Warren Buffett—but so do crazy loners with guns and the courage to carry out their plans. No place does home-turf nutjobs like America. American earnestness comes at a price.

The English, by contrast, are natural skeptics, but they, too, have a high tolerance for difference and tend to like people who are what they call "bloody-minded." Those who are "bloody-minded" are perverse, contrary, or stubborn, but the original and literal meaning was "bloodthirsty and inclined to violence." No wonder the two countries remain political allies. Former prime minister Tony Blair was loved—and hated—in equal measure by the English for his American-style charisma and overconfidence. He lent President Bush a bust of Winston Churchill shortly after the September 11 terrorist attacks, as if to assure Bush that they were in it together, for better or worse. Churchill—with his just war and his "never, never, never give up"—was a high compliment to an American president contemplating a war of his own. Churchill also said that one could "always count on Americans to do the right thing—after they've tried everything else," but it's probably safe to say that wasn't the quote on Blair's mind at the time.

The two nations went wholeheartedly down their path to war, and we all know how that turned out. In a television interview shortly after his presidency ended, Bush admitted that the flawed case for war in Iraq was his "biggest regret," saying, "That's a do-over that I can't do." But in the end, "The thing that's important for me is to get home and look in that mirror and say, 'I did not compromise my principles.'"

Unlike Miss Utah, he appears to have learned nothing. But at least he's OK with it.

Whinge

*In which the existence of the English "stiff upper lip"
is called into question.*

"Mustn't grumble" is a phrase as much associated with the English as "keep calm and carry on" or "keep a stiff upper lip." Like the Black Knight in *Monty Python and the Holy Grail*, who insists, upon having both arms cut off by King Arthur, that "'tis merely a scratch!" the English have a reputation for stoicism. So you might not expect that a word meaning "peevish complaint" has been in consistent use among them since the 1500s. That word is *whinge*—and actually, the English themselves would be the first to tell you that the stiff upper lip is not much in evidence anymore. The English grumble *all the time*. They make rather a point of it. Matthew Engel, writing for the *Financial Times Magazine*, identified "the Grumble" as a great British institution, noting that the phrase "contains that other very English quality, irony. It can be a disguised grumble. In fact, the English are very practiced and skilful grumblers . . . What they are bad at is complaining . . . They habitually refuse to tackle an issue head-on." (Interestingly, a common response to "How are you?" in England is "Can't complain.")

Whinging as a word carries with it a whiff of futility. Whinging is a passive occupation, whereas someone who complains might actually expect—and get—results. If you ever accidentally cut someone in a line in England (known as "jumping the queue"), what you'll hear will be grumbling, whinging, under-the-breath comments, and sighs: the barely audible sounds of half a dozen people deciding, all at once, not to confront you. Whereas an American might just say, "Hey, buddy—the end of the line is over there."

Americans, too, are great at whining—but when they want something to change, they complain. The English feel more comfortable with whinging than complaining because whinging is not considered too confrontational or high-maintenance. Whinging requires nothing more of the person listening than a nod, a shrug, or some other mild form of agreement. This can frustrate attempts to help them. On the BBC's consumer affairs call-in program, *You and Yours*, hosts Winifred Robinson and Peter White spend a substantial portion of each show trying to figure out—often cutting people off midwhinge—what their callers actually want them to *do*. For callers to a consumer affairs radio show, they are surprisingly unfocused on solving their problems and seem content with merely being heard. Still, England needs a show like *You and Yours*, as it focuses attention on the more egregious lapses in service by English companies.

Customer service is not what it might be in England—an ob-

vious and boring observation on a par with saying that there is a
lot of water in the Atlantic. In an article for *The New Yorker*,
"Take It or Leave It," the English author Zadie Smith, who lives
in New York, compares the American word *takeout* (which she
defines as food that a restaurant "intends to take out and deliver
to someone," though many Americans would be more likely use
the word *delivery*) with England's word, *takeaway*, which implies the eater should "come and take away your own bloody
food, thank you very much." Smith prefers the American model,
but takes issue with Americans' most common complaint about
England: "I'm not going to complain about Britain's 'lack of a
service culture' . . . I don't think any nation should elevate service to the status of culture. At best, it's a practicality, to be en-
acted politely and decently by both parties, but no one should be
asked to pretend that the intimate satisfaction of her existence
is servicing you, the 'guest,' with a shrimp sandwich wrapped in
plastic." But "intimate satisfaction" seems to me to be a vast
overstatement of Americans' expectations when it comes to service. Politeness and decency is really what it's about—and being
made to feel appreciated as a customer. Being treated well as a
customer, one feels inspired—or at the very least obligated—to
respond in kind, and ideally, respect and appreciation are mu-
tually reinforced. Is that too much to ask?

Service people in England tend to regard customers with
suspicion. In most English shops, the assumption that "the customer is always right" is nonexistent, even laughable. This
raises any store with great service to the level of consumer nir-
vana. These few, exceptional stores are celebrated, never taken
for granted as they might be in America. One example is the
chain department store John Lewis. An American who shall re-

main nameless bought the wrong size sheets (easy to do, as standard US and UK bed sizes differ by several inches), discovering the mistake only after discarding all the packaging and attempting to make the bed. He put the already-washed sheets back into the John Lewis bag and returned to the store, and the staff actually exchanged them—even sympathized with him. (You have to wonder if the sales assistants in the bed and bath department would have had such a kindly reaction to a woman who'd made the same silly mistake. Which is why I sent my husband to return the sheets.) Sometimes simply being American can work in a consumer's favor in England. If you are willing to confront an issue politely but directly, people will be so nonplussed that they'll often give you what you've asked for. Whereas whinging would be met with a shrug: "What you want me to do about it, mate?" One could argue that frustrating encounters like that positively require a stiff upper lip, but instead many English businesses and government offices need to display prominent signs saying things like, WARNING: WE WILL NOT TOLERATE PHYSICAL OR VERBAL ABUSE TOWARDS OUR STAFF. All right, then.

Given how good Americans are at complaining, and the emotional tenor of American life in general, I was amazed to find out that the phrase "stiff upper lip"—so strongly associated by Americans with the English—actually originated in the United States. Historian Thomas Dixon, in his "History of Emotions" blog, relates that the phrase was unknown to British readers as late as the 1870s: "It is a pleasing irony that it was introduced to them in a magazine founded by Charles Dickens, the great master of Victorian pathos and sentimentality. Dickens died in 1870. The following year, his journal *All the Year*

Round carried an article on 'Popular American Phrases' in which to 'keep a stiff upper lip' was explained as meaning 'to remain firm to a purpose, to keep up one's courage.' Even by the end of the nineteenth century the phrase still appeared in quotation marks, and was sometimes explained as an Americanism." The phrase came about at a time when life in America was "hard cheese," as my friend Peter likes to say. The first recorded use of the term was in 1815, when the nation was not quite forty years old, and it continued at least through the time of the Civil War, after which it was discovered by the English. As life became easier in America, this phrase and the implied stoic orientation to life slowly disappeared, in favor of a more emotionally open and honest style that is taken to extremes today.

The English were not always known for their stiff upper lips, any more than Americans are now. In the Victorian era and even before, public weeping by men and women alike was considered normal, and outpourings of public grief sometimes accompanied the deaths of public figures. As the editor of *Private Eye*, Ian Hislop, has observed, "In the 18th Century the word 'sentimental' was not pejorative in [England]. It was a term of praise for a person of taste and refinement who displayed their emotions openly. The nation which would become known for its ability to 'keep calm and carry on' had yet to appear."

This began to change near the end of the nineteenth century. Dixon cites Darwin's pioneering study, *The Expression of the Emotions in Man and Animals* (1872), which "popularized a racial hierarchy of emotional expression, with restrained Englishmen at the top and primitive 'savages' at the bottom. Darwin asserted that 'savages weep copiously from very slight causes,' whereas 'Englishmen rarely cry, except under the pressure of the acutest grief.' " The stiff upper lip reached its apotheosis with the wars of the twentieth century. As my father-in-law, who was born at the end of World War II, is wont to say in a crisis: "Worse things happen at sea," and he is mostly right. But this attitude is not common today, and some who were raised with it have abandoned it as the trait of their parents' generation. A study (somewhat oddly commissioned by Warburtons Family Bakers) found that seven out of ten people in England greet their friends with a double cheek kiss, six out of ten have wept in public, and eight out of ten cry in front of family and friends. Many have observed that the floodgates seemed to have been opened on or about August 31, 1997, as drifts of flowers were flung in front of Kensington Palace and much of the nation went into a very public period of mourning for Princess Diana. To be sure, not everyone abandoned their stiff upper lips during this time, but those who came out against the outpouring of grief, or admitted to finding it repellent, were all but censored.

Wistfulness for the stiff upper lip runs deep in England, as evidenced by the runaway success of the adage "Keep Calm and Carry On." This poster, with its cheery red background and crown logo, is assumed by many to have been a morale-booster during World War II. In fact, the British government's Ministry of Information had designed it specifically for use in the event of a Nazi occupation, and when the war ended, thousands of copies were pulped. One of the few still in existence surfaced in 2000, in a bookstore in the north of England called Barter Books. The owners, Stuart and Mary Manley, decided to sell reproductions. As Mary told *The New York Times*, it evokes a "nostalgia for a certain British character, an outlook." How the image is being used today reflects the massive cultural shifts since World

War II. The image has been thoroughly commodified—on products like mugs, tea towels, posters, pins, and tote bags—increasing in popularity even as the English populace appears less and less likely to heed its message. The situation is ripe for parody, and one alternative design, reading "Now Panic and Freak Out," seems more apropos.

Americans are equally besotted with the "Keep Calm and Carry On" meme (or, as one parody has it, "Meme meme and memey meme"). They persist in seeing the English in this old-fashioned way, possibly because the English are still quite aloof compared to them, and Americans understandably read this as stoicism. These days, while the English, for example, rarely speak to strangers on trains, feel slightly uncomfortable when someone holds more than one door in a row open for them, and generally give outsiders a wide berth, within their own social circles they can be just as dramatic, sentimental, and maudlin as anyone else. It's kind of refreshing—at least, you won't hear me whinging about it.

Bloody

In which we swear—and share—alike.

When Martin Scorsese's *The Wolf of Wall Street* was released in 2014, it had the questionable distinction of containing more F-bombs than any other drama—2.83 per minute, a total of 506. Only a documentary about the word itself, appropriately titled *Fuck*, exceeds it in cinematic history, with 857 instances. But this is far from unusual for American films, in which profane words frequently number in the hundreds. Television tends to have stricter standards. Back in 1972, the comedian George Carlin released an album including a monologue called "Seven Words You Can Never Say on Television." These days, you can hear all of them on cable, but they remain taboo for network television shows. This has inspired creativity. As Dan Harmon, the creator of *Community*, told *The New York Times*, "As a writer, you're always reaching for a more potent way to call somebody a jerk. [*Douche*] is a word that has evolved in the last couple of years—a thing that sounds like a thing you can't say."

The influence of American films and television on English culture is strong. Any English person who hasn't visited America could be forgiven for assuming that America is one giant cluster-cuss, its citizens dropping F-bombs like Eliza Doolittle dropped her *H*s. But this isn't necessarily so. There is a real puritanical streak in America that is much discussed—but little understood—by the English. It manifests itself in unpredictable ways, like an unwillingness to use seemingly innocuous words (see *Toilet*, page 55) and a certain gentility when it comes to swearing. For example, Americans consider it a big deal when a public figure is caught cussing. After President Obama declared his intention to "find out whose ass to kick" in connection with the BP oil spill, *Time* magazine published a "Brief History of Political Profanity," saying that although "the comment wasn't particularly vulgar . . . coarse language always seems shocking when it comes from the mouth of a President." Americans—even presidents—use all kinds of language, but in real life swearing retains more of its shock value than you would imagine, if your primary contact with American culture were its movies.

It is not unusual, in the real America, to meet a graduate of the Ned Flanders School of Swearing. "Gosh darn it!" "What the dickens?" "What the flood?" "Leapin' Lazarus!" Julie Gray, in her blog, "Just Effing," describes the phenomenon: "I recently said to someone that I'd be shocked as pink paint if something didn't happen. My mother used to describe either a person or a situation that was going downhill as 'going to hell in a hand basket.' My grandmother used to say 'good NIGHT' when something surprised or shocked her . . . I don't know where I picked it up but I will sometimes say 'H-E double toothpicks' or 'fudge.' " Even Nicholson Baker, in his book *House of Holes* (promisingly subtitled "A Book of Raunch"), has his characters say things like "for gosh sakes," "golly," and "damnation" as well as "fuck," just to keep it real.

Celia Walden, an English woman who moved to LA, described for the *Telegraph* her realization that Americans "don't use expletives as much as we do." She found it refreshing ("I haven't been cursed at in nearly a year") and noted that her "new sensitivity" to swearing might be related to having become a mother to a child whom she'd rather "didn't end up like the tiny mite I once saw fall out of his pushchair in Shepherd's Bush, look accusingly up at his mother, and calmly enunciate the words: 'Bloody hell.' I still wonder whether those were that poor child's first words."

No matter what age they start, the English seem far more fluent at swearing than Americans. They are more likely to link colorful language with having a sense of humor than with coarseness or vulgarity. Some even have the ability to make a word sound like a swear when it isn't. Stephen Fry and Hugh Laurie once performed a comedy sketch based on the idea that if the BBC wouldn't let them swear on the air, they'd simply make up their own curse words, "which are absolutely pitiless in their detail . . . and no one can stop us from using them. Here they are:

STEPHEN: Prunk.

HUGH: Shote.

STEPHEN: Cucking.

HUGH: Skank.

STEPHEN: Fusk.

HUGH: Pempslider.

STEPHEN: No, we said we wouldn't use that one.

HUGH: Did we?

STEPHEN: Yes, that's going too far.

HUGH: What, "pempslider"?

STEPHEN: Shut up.

Even without making up new words, the English definitely have, and make use of, a larger vocabulary of swears than Americans. Americans mostly find it funny—as if the English were swearing in another language—but Ruth Margolis, writing for BBC America's blog "Mind the Gap: A Brit's Guide to Surviving America," warned them that Americans might find their language offensive: "To get on in polite company, try to avoid . . . friendly-offensive banter. Brits exchange jovial insults because we're too uptight and emotionally stunted to say how we really feel. The stronger your friendship, the more you can lay into each other and still come away with a warm feeling. This is not how Americans roll. Tell your U.S. pal he's a moron, a twat or a daft f***, and you likely won't get invited to his wedding."

Indeed, there are some words the English use casually that are considered more offensive or insulting by Americans. As Margolis notes, for example, in England one might plausibly tease a friend of either sex by calling them a *twat* (rhymes with *cat*) or the four-letter *c*-word, which is all but unsayable in the United Sates—and which linguist John McWhorter (while not at all against swearing in principle) has lumped in with the *n*-word as one of Americans' most taboo. Americans find it really shocking to hear it used carelessly.

There are also words the English use that are actually "swearier"—even less polite—than they sound to the American ear, simply because they are unfamiliar. Hugh Grant gets a huge laugh saying, "Bugger! Bugger!" to express frustration in *Four Weddings and a Funeral*, but, as Philip Thody describes in *Don't Do It! A Dictionary of the Forbidden, bugger* is a term of bigotry and abuse with a long and nasty history: "Rarely used in a literal sense in modern English, and scarcely used at all in the USA, where the term is sodomy . . . It comes, through the Old French 'bougre,' from the attitude of the Roman Catholic Church in the Middle Ages to the Greek Orthodox Church, whose members were said to be Bulgarians, infected by the Albigensian heresy, and thus tending to practise unnatural vices. Since the Cathars made a special virtue of chastity, it was a shade unfair. However, since in the Middle Ages sodomy and buggery were linked to heresy as well as to witchcraft, it was perhaps only to be expected." *Bugger* is also versatile: "Bugger off" means "go away." "I'll be buggered" is a general expression of surprise. "Bugger me!" is as well, but it implies a greater degree of astonishment. Similarly, the word *sod*— used to describe a foolish person, or to tell someone to "sod off" (get lost)—is actually short for *sodomite*.

Bloody is an all-purpose intensifier that, according to the *Oxford English Dictionary*, once qualified as the strongest expletive available in just about every English-speaking nation except the United States. In 1914 its use in George Bernard Shaw's *Pygmalion* was hugely controversial. (Later, when a reporter from the *Daily Express* interviewed an actual Cockney flower girl, she said that Shaw's dialogue was unrealistic: Neither she nor her fellow flower-floggers would ever have used such a filthy word.) When Gilbert and Sullivan's opera *Ruddigore*—originally spelled *Ruddygore*—opened in January 1887, the title caused considerable offense. Ian Bradley relates in *The Complete Annotated Gilbert & Sullivan* that W. S. Gilbert, when approached by a member of his London club who commented that he saw no difference between "Ruddygore" and "Bloodygore," shot back, "Then I suppose you'll take it that if I say 'I admire your ruddy countenance,' I mean 'I like your bloody cheek.'" It's hard to take *bloody* seriously now, given how often the English use it. This is the risk with any good swear: Overuse it and it loses its meaning. Still, to Americans *bloody* remains the quintessential English swear, and one of the only ones they have not adopted themselves (except when they're being pretentious or ironic).

Both countries share a fascination with swears that reference the male anatomy. Americans and the English have *dick*, *cock*, and *prick* in common, but England takes the theme further with *pillock* and *knob*, as well as *masturbator* synonyms *tosser* and *wanker*. A commenter named Brian D. on Ben Yagoda's blog, "Not One-Off Britishisms," told the story of a group of British engineers from his company, sent to work at Wang Labs in Massachusetts. They were asked to attend a meeting to recognize an employee for outstanding achievement: "It was announced from the stage that this person was a King in the company and so would be presented with the Wang King award. The entire British contingent had to leave the room in hysterics."

Misunderstandings abound, but one thing is for sure. If you choose to swear, and you want your swearing to be understood on both sides of the Atlantic, you can't go wrong with the classic, the universal, the little black dress of swears: *fuck*. As Audrey Hepburn once said, "Everything I learned, I learned from the movies."

Scrappy

*In which we recognize the difference between American-
and English-style self-deprecation.*

Sticks and stones may break your bones, but words can get you into real trouble. Whether you mean to insult or compliment, you'd better first make sure that the word you choose means what you think it means. For example, if something is cozy and comfortable in England it might be called homely. In America, *homely* means ugly. In England, a muppet is a foolish or incompetent person. In America, a muppet is a character from the beloved TV show by Jim Henson. Someone (or something) described as scrappy in England is untidy or poorly organized, whereas in America, someone who is scrappy is determined to win or achieve something, often in spite of mitigating circumstances. In America, *scrappy* is a compliment that carries the connotation of the underdog.

There is something unseemly about American-style scrappiness to the English—it smacks of trying too hard—but England has a well-deserved reputation for loving and supporting the underdog, especially in sport (a word the English do not automatically pluralize, as Americans do). Although the English claim to have invented every sport worth playing, these days they are tops only at cycling. They have become used to their players being underdogs at nearly everything else. So when an English athlete or team wins, there is a bit of hand-wringing in the lead-up to the victory, followed by unbridled joy. Maybe winning means more to the English than they would like to admit—and who could blame them? The overdog of the nineteenth century is still coming to terms with its reduced circumstances in the twenty-first.

Americans have an international reputation for favoring winners, yet there is not much Americans like more than an underdog. It may be hard for an outsider to square America's overdog status with an appreciation for the downtrodden, but to Americans it makes sense. A great deal of America's self-mythology is about overcoming adversity. From the triumph of the American Revolution to tales of pioneers settling the West to prospectors seeking their fortunes in the unforgiving tundra of Alaska, the narrative of the unlikely victory is central to American history. America may be the overdog of the twenty-first century, but the memory of those earlier underdog times is still strong. That's why Americans prefer their winners to be underdogs, and will often cast a player as an underdog in order to make his win the sweeter. The idea that an underdog competitor is scrappier—that he tries harder—is corroborated by Malcolm Gladwell in his book *David and Goliath: Underdogs, Misfits, and the Art of Battling Giants*, in which he recounts stories of unlikely winners and how their grit and determination, along with an outsider's perspective, give them a counterintuitive competitive advantage.

In America, unlike England, this love of scrappiness and underdoggery transcends the sporting arena. Americans, individually (though not collectively), like to portray themselves as underdogs, and are apt to share their stories of struggle on the slightest provocation. A successful entrepreneur may confess he is dyslexic. You might find out that someone is still identifying with a formerly persecuted ethnic minority (Italian-American, Irish-American) even though they are the fourth generation born in New Jersey/Boston and their primary connection with that background is Mama's meatballs/soda bread. A well-off financial consultant might tell you that when he was a child, his parents barely had food on the table the week before payday. From working the night shift to fast-talking their way into a first job in their field to subsisting for months on Top Ramen, Americans are proud—not embarrassed—to tell you what they have had to do to get to where they are. It proves that they are hard and diligent workers, that they are scrappy. (When I moved to New York just after college, I got a second job at a bakery to subsidize my dream of becoming a book editor. I'd spend my weekends selling muffins by day and reading manuscripts late into the night. This lasted until one memorable Sunday when, too tired for precision, I accidentally sliced the tip of my finger off with a breadknife and ended up in the emergency room, in tears of pain but also rather proud of my work ethic.) Americans are always on the make, and they don't mind who knows it. The self-mythologizing starts early, often long before the college application essays are due. Americans—particularly successful ones—want to be seen as self-made, to the point of oversharing about their struggles. English love of the underdog doesn't go quite so far.

In England, to be called scrappy (in the American sense) would not be a compliment at all. There is no shame in being self-made (except to the old-school snob), but there isn't any glory in it, either. The English are not keen to broadcast their backgrounds and personal history. It would be gauche to be seen to compete, to be seen to care too much about winning, or to ask—or answer—direct questions about one's origins. Julian Fellowes, creator of *Downton Abbey*, is a particularly keen observer of this English trait. In his novel *Snobs*, he describes a character of the upper class, the Earl of Broughton: "He did not question nor resist his position but neither did he exploit it. If he had ever thought about the issues of inheritance or rank he would only have said that he felt very lucky. He would not have said this aloud, however." Of another, Lady Uckfield, he writes: "It pleased [her] always to give the impression that everything in life had been handed to her on a plate."

Even to put out a hand in greeting can feel too pushy for some, like Evelyn Waugh's Lady Metroland ("Out of Depth"), who "seldom affronted her guests' reticence by introducing them." This does not mean that the English are any less curious about the answer to the question "Where y'all from?" than Americans. But because their social conventions prevent them from asking it, they have to rely on clues. When the English meet one another, they engage in a complicated dance. To the outsider they may appear to be talking about the weather, but actually they are doing what dogs do when they sniff one another's bottoms: They are figuring out if they can be friends.

The song "Why Can't the English" from *My Fair Lady* may be antiquated, but it isn't incorrect: "An Englishman's way of speaking absolutely classifies him / The moment he talks he makes some other Englishman despise him." Accent is the first—but not the most important—clue. Occupation, education, address, cultural references, and income also count—but all of these things have to be ascertained indirectly. Where there is a large disparity, scrupulous politeness most often rules the day. The smaller disparities are what bring out the withering snobbery that can characterize some of these collisions.

Self-deprecation, the English art of one-downsmanship, often plays a role in the classification ritual. Middle- and upper-middle-class women excel at this, and will bond with one another (or not) by volunteering negative details about themselves, their homes, even their children—defects that usually cannot be discerned by the naked eye. This can be genuine (among friends and equals) or ironic, and sometimes it's not easy for an outsider to tell the difference. Consider this example. A woman whose children were at school with the Middleton children was quoted by the *Daily Mail*, seeming to compliment their immaculate appearance while denigrating that of her own brood: "Every pristine item of clothing would have a beautifully sewn-in name tape . . . unthinkable that they'd end up resorting to marker pens on labels like the rest of us. There were huge picnics at sports day, the smartest tennis racquets, that kind of thing. It made the rest of us all feel rather hopeless." Don't be fooled. By offering evidence that the Middletons cared about appearances, and lavished cash on fancy clothes and kit, this mother is establishing her own upper-class bona fides (secure enough to let her kids look rumpled, and name tags be damned) while condemning the Middletons as strivers and try-hards of middle rank, at best. If she'd actually considered the Middletons part of her social class, she would not have isolated them from the herd with the telling term "the rest of us." This brand of irony is usually lost on Americans, for good reason: Who wouldn't want to be the faultless family at the school picnic? Now you know.

Another notorious diss took place between Tory politicians in 1987, and was recorded by the MP and diarist Alan Clark. Michael (Lord) Jopling, at the time Minister of Agriculture, said of Michael Heseltine, who had recently—and contentiously— resigned from Margaret Thatcher's cabinet, "The trouble with Michael is that he had to buy all his furniture." Heseltine was no favorite with the "pinkish toffs" who considered him an "arriviste," according to Clark, who sneered, "all the nouves [sic] in the Party think he is the real thing." While still an undergraduate, Heseltine was said to have sketched out his life's goals on the back of an envelope (millionaire by twenty-five; MP by thirty-five; prime minister by fifty-five). He claims no memory of this, but as Decca Aitkenhead reported in *The Guardian*, while Heseltine fell short of his ultimate goal, "the envelope has become parliamentary shorthand for the vulgar hubris of ambition." Ironically, Heseltine is today as firm a member of the political Establishment as it would be possible to be without having been PM. A footnote: One of Alan Clark's Tory peers felt his glee at Jopling's remark was "a bit rich coming from a person whose father had to buy his own castle."

I don't mean to give the impression that England abhors the self-made. It's immodesty that rankles. Those who court publicity, flaunt their wealth, or maintain high profiles risk a strong backlash. The public fascination with men like Alan Sugar (Donald Trump's opposite number on the English version of *The Apprentice*) and Richard Branson, the founder of Virgin, is not just due to their bootstrapping and vast fortunes, but to their lack of humility. They are upfront to the point of chippiness, as in "chip on the shoulder." They are brash and indiscreet, and this is why they routinely come in for a bashing by the press. When Branson relocated to his tax-free Caribbean island, Necker, citing health—and not wealth—as his reason, sniping ensued. In the *Daily Mirror*, Brian Reade said, "[He should] change his title from Knight of the Realm to Pirate of the Caribbean." Still, one gets the sense that Sugar and Branson, and others like them, are polarizing on purpose. They don't much care what the Establishment thinks and they relish their role in public life. They seem to be having a lot of fun. And I'm fairly sure that neither would take it as an insult if an American called him scrappy.

Pull

In which we close our eyes and think of England.

magine for a moment you are learning English as a foreign language. What would you make of words and phrases like *pull*, *snog*, *pick up*, *make out*, and *screw*? Do these sound like events in the World's Strongest Man competition? Lesser-known Olympic sports? Things that might happen at a Monster Truck Rally? (SUNDAY! SUNDAY! SUNDAY! BE THERE! BE THERE! BE THERE!) Courtship slang in English is anything but dignified. Of course, there are words in English for perfectly innocent activities, like retrieving golf balls from practice ranges, that are just as strange. Does *ball shagging* sound like something it ought to be legal to pay a young boy to do?

Pull, *snog*, and *shag* are the English synonyms for *pick up*, *make out*, and *screw*. *Pulling*—attracting someone—is the point of a singles night out and "Did you pull?" the morning-after question among friends, though the word isn't specific about what the puller and the "pullee" actually did together. In that way it's similar to America's term *hooking up*, which can mean snogging or shagging or both. Americans also use baseball metaphors for sex, with first base, second base, third base, and fourth base corresponding to increasing levels of intimacy, from kissing to intercourse. The English haven't tried this with cricket. Given that one game can last up to five days, it's probably for the best. To fancy someone, in English English, is to have a romantic attraction to him or her. (Heads up, though—you can also fancy some cake, a new pair of shoes, or a cup of tea in a wholly platonic way.) If you chat someone up, you're probably hoping for a snog. A less precious way to communicate attraction for someone of either sex is the English equivalent of a wolf whistle (and about as welcome): *Phwoarr!*

Shag is a word most Americans know from Mike Myers's series of James Bond spoofs, including *Austin Powers: The Spy Who Shagged Me*. *Shag* is a far coarser word in its native land than one would guess from watching these movies. The sexual humor is so adolescent the films could almost have been written by a teenage boy, if they didn't contain so many knowing references to popular comedians of the 1960s, like Benny Hill and Peter Sellers. It may be true that the more serious the subject, the more likely the English are to be joking. There is a pervasive pubescent tone to much of English sexual politics. In what other country could you put a topless woman on page three of a daily newspaper (the *Sun* is the UK's bestselling daily newspaper, though the editors of the *Daily Telegraph* like to point out that theirs is the UK's bestselling *quality* daily newspaper) and have it be considered, in the words of *Sun* editor Dominic Monahan, an "innocuous institution"? Don't fret, America, it's not as smutty as it sounds. One of page three's models, Peta Todd, has said, "You'd struggle to find anything very sexual on Page 3, it's quite kitsch. If the picture is too sexy, if it's not smiley, the people who get the most upset are the *Sun* readers." Not that Americans are so mature. They are the ones who made the Austin Powers series such a hit in the first place, and they think underwear models are even sexier when they are wearing huge angel wings.

When it comes to dating, there are some major differences in approach. Americans are more likely to go on casual dates with people they have just met. Some dating experts even advocate a "one-date rule"—in other words, always saying yes to a first date, regardless of your first impression of a person, because *you never know*. When Americans meet someone they want to get to know better, they will not necessarily stop seeing other people—until they have had "the talk" in which they decide to become an exclusive, official couple.

Americans are quick to admit interest and slower to commit to a relationship. By contrast, the English are slow to admit interest but much quicker to assume exclusivity once it is requited. An American friend who moved to England described the tortuous line of indirect questioning she would be subjected to—at the end of a party or a night at the pub—by men who had no intention of asking her out on a date. They'd want to know exactly how she came to be there, who her other friends were, what part of town she lived in, and how long she was staying—just for a start. She finally figured out that they were trying to ascertain the likelihood of running into her again without actually making plans with her directly, not out of laziness, but because to register a particular interest was too high-stakes for them. She would have to run into someone (orchestrated or not, who knows) half a dozen times before he might ask her to dinner. By then, he would assume she wasn't "seeing" anyone else at the same time. And once they'd had a successful date or two, they'd already be considered an item—even without having an American-style exclusivity talk. She found out the hard way that her casual, American attitude to dating did not translate in England.

These cultural differences seem to run deeper than the usual assumptions about English reticence and American extroversion. In fact, you don't even have to be on the pull to know this is true. An American or English expat will figure it out just by trying to make friends. About a year after we moved to England, we had a dinner party, and on this night we learned something (other than how much wine people can consume before they become combative or pitch face-first into their pudding—the usual lessons of a London dinner party).

A colleague of my husband's asked me how I liked London. I said I liked it very much, but was having a hard time getting past initial polite conversations, converting acquaintances into friends. He said he wasn't surprised, "because England is a small town." He explained that whether you live in a small town or a large city in England, you rarely have more than a few degrees of separation from people you are likely to date or become friends with: Imagine if everyone you knew from childhood, school, and university ended up in the same handful of places, none of them very far apart. Dating in England is dating in a small town—regardless of whether you are doing it in Bourton-on-the-Water or Birmingham, London or Leamington. It's a small country made even smaller by class divisions.

Dating in America is only like dating in a small town if you actually live in a small town, or if you rarely leave your immediate context (your office, your gym, or your apartment block) in a big city. In *Seinfeld*'s "The Pool Guy" episode, George objects to his friend Elaine befriending his girlfriend, Susan, and rants about his "worlds colliding":

GEORGE: You have no idea of the magnitude of this thing. If she is allowed to infiltrate this world, then George Costanza as you know him ceases to exist. You see, right now I have Relationship George. But there is also Independent George. That's the George you know, the George you grew up with . . . Movie George, Coffee Shop George, Liar George, Bawdy George.

JERRY: I, I love that George.

GEORGE: Me too. And he's dying, Jerry. If Relationship George walks through this door, he will kill Independent George. A George divided against itself cannot stand!

George may be a particularly vehement example, but this is funny to Americans precisely because many have had a milder version of the same thought. An American would not necessarily expect—or want—all of his friends to know one another. This might seem odd to the English, many of whom take for granted a lifetime's worth of friends—and the friends of those friends—

living within a few miles and comprising a coherent inner circle. The social risks involved in pulling in an outsider can
outweigh the benefits, and even if not, the stakes are certainly
higher than they would be in a much bigger country, with a more
atomized population, like the United States. This explains why
there is so much less random, *You seem nice, let's have coffee*
dating in England. And it is one reason why American expatriates in England can seem so insular. Expat friends are easily
made, and the stakes are quite low—people are always moving
on, leaving a vacuum to be filled by another new arrival. It's
much harder to cultivate a new English friend who has to run
into you at half a dozen gatherings before they feel they know
you well enough to commit to a one-on-one meeting. The search
for platonic friends takes on a real urgency when you move to a
new country, not unlike the search for a life partner. I have come
to think of coffee as "first base." "Second base" is lunch. "Third
base" is being invited to dinner at their home, and a home run is
when they decide to go all the way and introduce you to their
other friends. With any luck, after a while you become close
enough that neither of you remembers who pulled whom.

Shall

*In which a word seldom heard in America
still speaks to the English.*

hall has all but disappeared from American English. If an American uses *shall* it is usually in an effort to sound more formal or to take what the English would call a "softly-softly" approach with someone. *Shall* survives in the service industry—"Shall I take your coat?"—and in fairy tales like *Cinderella*: "You *shall* go to the ball, my dear."

Shall denotes obligation and necessity rather than choice; it's the "have to" to *will*'s "want to." In everyday speech, *shall* strikes Americans as having what H. L. Mencken called a "pansy cast."

Indeed, for the benefit of anyone who isn't clear on the distinction (you're in good company), here's the rule:

For simple futurity, use *shall* after *I* or *we*, but *will* after everything else:

> *I shall get help. We shall get help.* (Whether we like it or not, help is coming.)

> *They will get help.* (No need to do anything; help is coming.)

To express determination or command, use *will* after *I* or *we* but *shall* after everything else:

> *I will get help. We will get help.* (My/our intention is to go and get help.)

> *They shall get help.* (They've been ordered to go and get help).

It is far simpler to substitute *will*. What's more, its connotations of the deliberate determination, rather than inevitability, of the future, chime with Americans' beliefs about how the world ought to work. It is part laziness, part vigor, that has killed *shall* in America. If you want to be a stickler about it, any book you consult will likely put the issue of *shall* vs. *will* to rest in two pages or fewer. Grammar Girl dispatches it in less than a page, with one caveat: "if you use *shall* in the British way during normal conversation, you might end up sounding pretentious or haughty."

In England, it is far more complicated and always has been. One of the more thorough prescriptions for the use of *shall* vs. *will*, in H. W. Fowler's *The King's English*, runs to twenty-two pages, and begins with a here-be-dragons: "It is unfortunate that the idiomatic use, while it comes by nature to southern Englishmen (who will find most of this section superfluous), is so complicated that those who are not to the manner born can hardly acquire it; and for them, the section is in danger of being useless." Although social class cannot be conflated with region, as Fowler seems to do here, his point remains: Here are twenty pages' worth of ways—based on a single word—to keep the lower classes in their place.

In England, no one wants to be seen to try too hard. Skills must come naturally, and seem effortless, in order to count. One mustn't be a plodder or a swot (grind), but come up with the goods while appearing not to care too much. This is particularly true of intellectual pursuits, but the rule extends to sports. The 1960s comedy duo Flanders and Swann sang of foreigners that "they argue with umpires, they cheer when they've won / And they practice beforehand, which ruins the fun."

Should an English person appear to make an embarrassing effort, and rise too far above his peers, vulnerability to attack is his reward. "Congratulations!" they'll say, with knives behind their backs. This is known as tall poppy syndrome, because, as an English friend explained, the tallest poppy is the one you want to cut first.

In America, effort (and, above all, being seen to make an effort) is practically a religion. In a 2011 study by the Pew Research Center, in which Americans were asked whether success in life is determined by forces outside their control, only 36 percent agreed. So perhaps it isn't surprising that *shall* is not really part of Americans' vocabulary. For them it is all about the individual *will*.

Americans persist in thinking they can be, do, or have anything they want if they work hard enough. This may not be strictly true in America these days; nevertheless it's an idea that runs deep in the American psyche and attests to the power the American Dream still holds.

Americans love and celebrate the successful. Not because jealousy doesn't exist, but because success for one gives hope to all. Nothing feels like a zero-sum game in an enormous country founded on the ideals of life, liberty, and the pursuit of happiness. The sentiment is *I want what she has* rather than *I don't want her to have what she has*. To the extent that an American believes those who rise above the rest deserve it, he is happy to see them as inspirations for dreams of his own limitless possibilities. After all, he could be next. It is only when he perceives that someone has cheated or swindled his or her way to the top that he sharpens the scissors.

An Englishman without a native understanding of *shall* vs. *will* should emigrate to America, where he will have a swell time indeed. If you doubt that Americans project such sterling qualities as authority, a sense of humor, and a refined intellect onto anyone who comes equipped with any sort of British accent, you haven't been there lately.

The English who are capable of deploying *shall* without making Fowler turn in his grave may be in the minority, but they are a powerful minority. Should you wish to join them, you might try using a helpful mnemonic devised by William Ward in 1765:

> The verb by *shall*, States of fixed order shows;
> Or States which Chance directs, as we suppose.
> And *shall* those verbal Future States declares
> Which *for itself*, an Object hopes or Fears,

Thinks *of itself*, surmises, or foresees;

But which for other objects it decrees.

The verb by *will* those Future States declares

For others, which an Object hopes or fears,

Of others thinks, surmises or foresees;

But *for itself*, States which itself decrees.

Confused?

The distinction between *shall* and *will* is breaking down even in England, and it's no mystery why. Imagine the plight of the non-native speaker, contemplating a beam so narrow that even the English themselves do not always stick the landing. The younger and more international the crowd, the more likely they are to avoid the issue altogether by using contractions, or substituting *will*. *Shall* isn't dead yet, though. Just two months after starting at an English nursery school, my daughter asked, "When shall we go to the park? Shall I get the umbrella?" I guess there are worse habits she could have picked up. In some English schools they still teach little girls to curtsy.

The attitude underlying *shall* endures although the upper-class credentials that redound to those who get it right are becoming less important, even to those who belong to the class in question. Anyone looking down his nose at someone for misusing *shall* in England today would be considered something worse than a stickler. Still, those who care might counter that while English may be perfectly intelligible without *shall*, any form of English that doesn't include it will be the poorer.

Sir

*In which the great and the good get gongs (and I explain
what that means, in English).*

t is our wedding day and people are all dressed up. Our American guests, having heard that the English contingent would be there, have made an effort with hats, like something out of a Richard Curtis movie. Most of the English guests have elected to leave their hats at home. It's Cambridge, Massachusetts, not Cambridgeshire. But it is all taking place during the day, so many of the men are wearing morning suits—even my father, who prefers flip-flops. I am ridiculously young, and getting away with a pouf of white silk and a veil attached to what the English romantically call an "Alice band," because Alice wore one in the Tenniel illustrations for Lewis Carroll's *Through the Looking Glass*. To me it is a headband.

I compliment an older gentleman, whom I've never met before, on his tie. He says, "Thank you, darling. My wife gave it to me when I was ninety." I say, "Really? But you don't look a day over seventy-five." He says, "No, darling, *knighted*!" We both laugh and I'm not sure who is more pleased. To me, he might as well be a member of the royal family. Actually, his title has been awarded on merit—as are most titles in England nowadays.

Twice each year—on New Year's Day and on the queen's birthday in June—the Cabinet Office publishes the Queen's Honours List, "marking the achievements and service of extraordinary people across the UK." There is a baffling array of orders within which honors may be awarded, depending on the type of service one has rendered to crown and country. These include (among others) the Order of the Bath, for senior civil servants and military officers (so named because of the ritual washing, symbolizing spiritual purification, that took place in late medieval times before investiture ceremonies); the Order of St. Michael and St. George, for diplomats and those who have served the UK abroad; the Royal Victorian Order, for people who have served the queen or the monarchy personally; the Order of the Garter, a rarefied order reserved for the king and twenty-five knights who have held public office or contributed in a meaningful way to national life; and the Order of the British Empire, which recognizes distinguished service to the arts and sciences, public services outside the Civil Service, and work with charitable and welfare organizations.

Within each order there are different ranks conferring gradations of prestige. For example, within the largest order, the Order of the British Empire, these are the MBE (member of the Order of the British Empire), for service that sets an example to others; the OBE (officer of the OBE), for a distinguished regional role in any field; the CBE (commander of the OBE), for work with a national impact; and finally the KBE/DBE (knight/dame commander of the OBE). To receive a knighthood or be made a dame, one has to have made a significant and inspirational contribution at a national level. Prominent people have been known to turn down honors that they did not feel were of a sufficiently exalted rank. Alfred Hitchcock turned down a CBE, but later accepted a knighthood. Evelyn Waugh also turned down a CBE in the hope of later being offered a knighthood, which, as it turned out, was not forthcoming.

Although it is the queen who bestows the honors, the Cabinet Office Honours and Appointments Secretariat handles the nominations at home, while the Foreign Office is responsible for the Diplomatic Service and Overseas List. Nominations may come from anyone, and there are nine independent committees who consider applications and make recommendations to the central honors committee before sending a list to the queen via the prime minister. It all sounds surprisingly corporate. The process is also competitive—so competitive, in fact, that many hopefuls pay specialist consultants to prepare their applications. The website for one of these organizations, Awards Intelligence, reads like a classier version of an ad for a personal injury attorney: "Are you ready for a queen's honour nomination? . . . Do you know someone who may be deserving of a queen's honour but you don't know if they meet all the right criteria? . . . Do you want your nomination to have the best possible chance of success in the Queen's Honours List? If you answered 'yes' to one or more of these questions contact us today."

When the long-awaited lists are released, inevitably it is the actors, footballers, and entertainers who receive the most publicity. But the overwhelming majority of those who get these coveted prizes, or "gongs," as the English call them, are not famous. The official website of the British monarchy notes that they could be charity volunteers, members of the emergency services or armed forces, industrial pioneers, or specialists in various professions. A prestigious award from the queen helps draw attention to their work and increase support for their causes. A friend who knows several recent OBE award-winners said that even the lefties (and ostensible antiroyalists) among them gushed about the experience of meeting the queen, and actually teared up when describing how proud their mothers were. It is also a huge ego boost, whether one likes to admit it or not. A gag in the popular 1980s political sitcom *Yes Minister* illustrates the point. Jim Hacker, the minister for administrative affairs, has asked his private secretary, Bernard, to explain the abbreviations for honors emanating from the Foreign Office (all under the Order of St. Michael and St. George):

BERNARD: . . . in the service, CMG stands for Call Me God. And KCMG for Kindly Call Me God.

HACKER: What about GCMG?

BERNARD: God Calls Me God.

Other titles exist in England, of course. There is the peerage, with ranks in descending order from duke, to marquess, earl, viscount, and baron. But today these titles are relics—like classic cars passed down from father to son—since only four new nonroyal hereditary peerages have been created since 1964 (and two went to men with no sons). The Life Peerages Act of

1958, in a very English gesture toward egalitarianism, made it possible to confer a life peerage on an accomplished individual without giving his heirs the right to the title in perpetuity. Membership in the House of Lords ceased to be automatic for peers in the late nineties anyway, so these titles now derive most of their cachet from reflected glory (and, of course, *HELLO!* magazine).

The word *knight* originally carried the sense of a servant or soldier, and service is still central to what it means to be a knight or a dame. People from other nationalities—even Americans—can be given honorary knighthoods. Bill Gates, former New York City mayor Rudolph Giuliani, presidents Reagan and George H. W. Bush, and Steven Spielberg are among those who have received this honor. But honorary knights are not "dubbed" with the sword by the queen, and they are not permitted to style themselves "Sir." Where's the fun in that?

Being known as "Sir" apparently can be more trouble than it is worth. Alistair Cooke, author of the popular *Letter from America* radio broadcast—weekly talks on American life that aired between 1946 and 2004—met a knighted actor who, having moved to Hollywood, complained that American service providers assumed his title meant he was "a very wealthy lord with twenty thousand acres . . . so where I normally gave a quarter tip I had to give a dollar and . . . where the car parking attendant used to get a dollar, now, unless I give him five, he positively sneers and mutters 'cheapskate.' " Cooke (who had given up his British citizenship) was later awarded an honorary knighthood himself, for his outstanding contributions to Anglo-American understanding.

The royal family is the source of all titles and the seat of he-

reditary privilege in England. Americans tend to be less critical
and (if anything) more fascinated by the royals than the English. Cynics would say that is at least partly because Americans
are not being taxed for their upkeep, unlike the English. England's antimonarchists (somewhat confusingly known as republicans) would like to abolish the whole business, and the Queen's
Honours are just one manifestation of the nobility that they sneer
at. Numerous nonrepublicans have turned down honors in the
past for reasons other than snobbery, whether in protest or because they simply didn't want the attention or the title—these include C. S. Lewis, David Hockney, Nigella Lawson, the comedy
duo French and Saunders, Roald Dahl, and J. G. Ballard, who
called the Honours system a "preposterous charade." It isn't un-
common for someone to be criticized for accepting a knighthood—
especially if it seems at odds with his public persona. Keith
Richards was apoplectic when Mick Jagger was knighted in 2003,
calling the honor "bollocks" and saying (among other, less-
printable things), "It's not what the Stones is about, is it?"

Still, about 80 percent of Britons approve of the monarchy.
And, as Olga Khazan reported in *The Atlantic*, the royal family—
while born to their titles—works quite hard representing the
UK. According to the British tourism agency, the royal family
generates close to five hundred million pounds in revenue per
year. Their estimated cost to the taxpayer likely falls somewhere
between Buckingham Palace's estimate of 33.3 million pounds
(or fifty-three pence per person) and the republicans' estimate
of two hundred million pounds per year. Either way, the royal
family looks like a bargain. More than most members of modern society, they could be said to be "in service": giving up any
semblance of a normal life and their privacy, spending most of

their time attending official events, and having to appear flawless in public at all times, without complaint. Not everyone is equal to that level of scrutiny, and it is more than most of us would be willing to put up with. Even so, like anyone refusing a knighthood or other honor from the queen, they must know that many others would gladly take their place.

As for my cousin by marriage, Bill Cotton, who had been knighted for his roles as head of light entertainment at the BBC and vice president of the Marie Curie Cancer Care charity, he died a few years ago. His memorial service packed St. Martin-in-the-Fields to the rafters, and no one noticed, I'm sure, that my American mother-in-law and I were among the only ones wearing hats. We'd assumed (embarrassingly? touchingly?) that hats would be the done thing. But we were so honored to be counted among Sir Bill's family, friends, and admirers: some of them knighted, some ninety, others not a day over seventy-five.

Yankee

In which we delve into the origins of a controversial nickname and uncover its unexpected relationship to pie.

T o the English, all Americans are Yankees. An American can usually tell, depending on the context and the speaker, whether or not the term is being used affectionately. *Yankee* is a word with baggage—it's complicated. Within the United States, the word is more strictly defined. Only New Englanders living in Connecticut, Maine, New Hampshire, Vermont, Massachusetts, and Rhode Island are likely to be considered, or to call themselves, Yankees. And the nearer you get to the Yankees themselves, the narrower the definition becomes. E. B. White explained it well:

> To foreigners, a Yankee is an American.
> To Americans, a Yankee is a Northerner.

To Northerners, a Yankee is a New Englander.

To New Englanders, a Yankee is a Vermonter.

And in Vermont, a Yankee is somebody who eats pie for breakfast.

Of course, White meant the classic American double-crust fruit pie (and you might struggle to find an American who *hasn't* eaten pie for breakfast—especially the day after Thanksgiving). In England, a fruit pie is usually made with only a top crust, and if you see a double-crust pie it is more likely to be savory, containing pork or some other meat. Although the pie-for-breakfast line may seem like a joke to outsiders, Vermonters have taken it seriously enough. Act 15 of the 1999 session of the Vermont Legislature enshrined the importance of pie eating—and certain standards for how it ought to be done—as law:

> When serving apple pie in Vermont, a "good faith" effort shall be made to meet one or more of the following conditions:
> (a) with a glass of cold milk,
> (b) with a slice of cheddar cheese weighing a minimum of 1/2 ounce,
> (c) with a large scoop of vanilla ice cream.

Just as Americans can be doctrinaire about what is and isn't correct to serve with pie, they are very particular about who they do—and don't—consider to be a true Yankee. Linguist Mark Liberman, in the blog "Language Log," recalled that, during his childhood in rural eastern Connecticut, "it was understood that only some of the people in our village were called 'Yankees' . . .

Later on, I learned that these people were the descendents of the English immigrants who had settled the area in the late 17th century, but when I was six or so, the characteristics that I associated with 'Yankees' included keeping a few farm animals on the side, trapping to earn a little extra money from furs, making hooked rugs from old socks, and shooting at garden pests . . . Although I participated in such activities with friends and neighbors, mine was certainly not a Yankee family in the local sense, and so it still takes me aback when I realize that some Texan or Virginian regards me as a Yankee."

America may not have as long a history as England, but nevertheless there is a lot of snobbery about whose ancestors got there "first." (Native Americans, naturally, excepted.) *Mayflower* bragging rights accrue to the descendants of the earliest settlers from England, who are considered the bluest of the blue-blood Yankees. In a country without a nobility, this is as close as one can get. This may explain why some people go to extraordinary lengths to trace their lineage back to the original *Mayflower* passengers who landed in Plymouth, Massachusetts, in 1620, only about a quarter of whom survived long enough to reproduce. A cursory glance at the daunting application requirements for the Mayflower Society would be enough to discourage most of the estimated twenty to thirty million descendants; still, the society has about twenty-seven thousand members. But a Yankee wasn't—and still isn't—always admired. Experts disagree on the origin of the word *Yankee*, but one thing we know for sure is that who qualifies as a Yankee, and whether or not that person is being mocked, has always depended on who you ask.

Prior to the American Revolution, *Yankee* was an insult.

British soldiers had nothing but contempt for the soldiers of the American colonies, who seemed to them a ragtag army of amateurs. The song "Yankee Doodle Dandy," now familiar to all American children, was once sung by the English to tease their rivals: "Yankee Doodle went to town, riding on a pony. Stuck a feather in his cap and called it macaroni." *Doodle* was a synonym for a fool or a simpleton, and *macaroni* was what the dandies of the day were called in England. So the song describes a bumpkin—an object of ridicule without style or guile. To Americans, however, muddling through despite a lack of experience or equipment can be a point of pride (see *Scrappy*, page 151).

Robert Hendrickson, in *Yankee Talk: A Dictionary of New England Expressions*, describes the way Americans began to claim the term *Yankee*:

> It wasn't until the Battle of Lexington, the first battle of the Revolution in 1775, that New Englanders began applying the nickname *Yankee* to themselves, making it respectable. Soon after, the process of dignification began and the story about the Yankos Indians was invented. In this tale a mythical tribe of Massachusetts Indians are said to have been defeated by a band of valorous New Englanders. The defeated Yankos so admired the bravery of their victorious adversaries that they gave them their name, *Yankos*, which meant Invincibles, and was soon corrupted to "Yankees."

Another theory is that the word comes from the Cherokee word *eankke*, which means "coward." How embarrassing. Yet Hendrickson's anecdote shows the extent to which Americans wanted to take this moniker from their enemies and own it for themselves. It did help that they won the war. "Yankee Doodle" soon became a triumphal march, and was adopted as the country's first national anthem. It remains the state song of Connecticut. The plucky spirit of Americans was, for a time, known as "Yankee-doodle-dandeeism," and America itself nicknamed "Yankeedoodledom."

But that's far from the end of the story. Even within America, *Yankee* can still be an insult. During the Civil War era, Confederates used the word to describe Federalists and other Northerners on the opposite side of the conflict. It is said in the South that there are three types of Yankees: A Yankee is someone who was born and still lives in the North. A Damned Yankee is one who visits the South. And a Goddamned Yankee is one who moves there permanently. They may be joking, but the jokes occasionally have an edge that would surprise most foreigners. Even though the official North–South conflict ended a long time ago, antagonism remains. These days the division in American culture is more likely to be described in terms of politics—the red (Republican) states vs. the blue (Democratic) ones. A quick glance at the map confirms that the Yankee states are mostly blue, and the Southern states mostly red.

But regardless of their different political leanings, something Americans have in common is an abiding patriotism that is centered on the flag. All Americans grow up pledging allegiance to the flag each school day. In my elementary school, the pledge was led by the principal over a tinny loudspeaker so that the words all ran together, except for the part about God: "Ipledgeallegiance-totheflagoftheunitedstatesofamerica [audible breath] andto-therepublicforwhichitstands, One Nation [breath] Under GOD, INDIVISIBLE! Withlibertynjusticeferall." Each classroom had its own flag, right up front—as does every public building in America.

Americans' flag-waving tendencies baffle the English, who generally don't go in for that particular flavor of nationalism. They have no equivalent ritual to the Pledge of Allegiance, though like Americans, they do sing their national anthem, "God Save the Queen," at official events. England also has a similar North–South cultural divide—but whereas Yankees are considered the cultural elites in America, in England the cultural and political elites are usually based in the south. The north of England is less populous and less wealthy than the south, which is the seat of government power, making policies for the country as a whole. This can lead to resentment, especially when southern politicians are seen to be out of touch with northern realities. Condescension toward northern accents and cities persists, with southern accents and cities considered "posher" than northern ones. The north has historically been the industrial heart of the country—represented by the "dark satanic mills" in one of England's most popular hymns, "Jerusalem" (which Americans may remember from the movie *Chariots of Fire*). It seems inevitable that the south would appear overprivileged by comparison, but there isn't any one word that sums this up in the rest of the country.

The word *Yankee* may represent different things to different people, but if you ask an American to describe an individual who is a Yankee, you will get a cross between the caricature of Uncle Sam and a kind of pilgrim soul, given to aphorisms like:

> "The world is your cow. But you have to do the milking."

"Take care of the minutes and the hours will take care of themselves."

"In New England we have nine months of winter and three months of darned poor sledding."

The characteristics traditionally ascribed to true Yankees—including shrewdness, industry, economy (with words as well as money), individualism, practicality, ingenuity, dry wit, and stoicism—are qualities that have also been ascribed to the English. Unfortunately these old, good values are in short supply everywhere now. It may be true that Americans who embody these characteristics, who call themselves Yankees as a point of pride, have more in common with old England than they do with the rest of America. Yet I would argue that today's England has more in common, culturally, with the rest of America than with the England of old. But if that's too controversial, even the most irascible Yankee might agree with Frances Trollope, who had her own idea—yet another—of what it means to be one:

> The Yankee: In acuteness, cautiousness, industry and perseverance, he resembles the Scotch. In habits of frugal neatness, he resembles the Dutch . . . but in frank admission, and superlative admiration of all his own peculiarities, a Yankee is nothing else on earth but himself.

Skint

In which the money-talk taboo buckles under the weight of the recent recession.

Neither Americans nor the English like talking about money. It is a cliché on both sides of the Atlantic that most people, rich or poor, would prefer to talk about their sex lives than the contents of their wallets. Both societies equate money with power, status, prestige, esteem, and self-worth. So it isn't easy to say the words we say when we don't have enough: *broke* and *skint*. *Skint* comes from the word *skinned*, meaning flayed, exposed. It is an intense and visceral word, and while it means the same as *broke*, it sounds much harsher.

Americans and the English are raised to believe that talking about money is impolite. But their similar taboos against money talk had very different origins. In England, the money-talk taboo originated with the class system. To the upper class, whose fortunes consisted of inherited property, there was always a stigma against being "in trade," or having to work to earn money. One (ideally) already *had* all of one's money, and if not, one could never be considered a gentleman, no matter how rich. This may sound absurd to us today, but nevertheless it is one reason why most English people of all classes, even now, consider it vulgar to talk about money or show too much interest in it. Everyone keeps up the polite assumption that they all have just enough—to do otherwise would be not only potentially divisive, but immodest, reductive, intrusive, and embarrassing.

Kate Fox, an English anthropologist who has studied her countrymen, takes them to task for this: "It is clear that much of all this English squeamishness about money is sheer hypocrisy. The English are no less naturally ambitious, greedy, selfish or avaricious than any other nation—we just have more and stricter rules requiring us to hide, deny and repress these tendencies . . . The modesty we display is generally false, and our apparent reluctance to emphasize status differences conceals an acute consciousness of these differences."

This is not new. It was played for laughs by Jane Austen in the early 1800s. You can't move far in her novels without finding out who has merely "500 a year" and who has been reduced to driving around in a gig rather than a phaeton. It's taken for granted that money is unequal and that money matters—especially in matchmaking—though the characters who are seen to be openly ambitious rarely win at this game. Austen herself kept careful records of how much money she earned from her writing, and never married. But it's interesting that in her books, the greatest romantic outcome of all is to marry, for love, someone who also just happens to be rich. This is the case when

Emma Woodhouse marries George Knightley and when Elizabeth Bennet bags Mr. Darcy. Elizabeth's worry, upon telling her mother, is that Mrs. Bennet's jubilation will prove embarrassing. This worry is not unfounded. Mrs. Bennet crows:

> "Oh! my sweetest Lizzy! how rich and how great you will be! What pin-money, what jewels, what carriages you will have! . . . A house in town! Every thing that is charming!" This was enough to prove that her approbation need not be doubted: and Elizabeth, rejoicing that such an effusion was heard only by herself, soon went away. But before she had been three minutes in her own room, her mother followed her.
>
> "My dearest child," she cried, "I can think of nothing else! Ten thousand a year, and very likely more! 'Tis as good as a Lord."
>
> This was a sad omen of what her mother's behavior to the gentleman himself might be; and Elizabeth found that, though in the certain possession of his warmest affection, and secure of her relations' consent, there was still something to be wished for.

In America, being in trade has never been stigmatized. It is an article of faith that "everyone is in sales!" Americans expect to "always be closing," whatever their jobs. Being self-made is, if anything, considered more honorable and better than being an heir. The rich worry about their children *not* having to make their own way in the world and try to instill character by other means. (A whole industry has built up around this—wealthy children are sent to summer sailing camps to learn self-reliance, or Outward Bound drops them in the middle of the wilderness to fend for themselves; some even endure unpaid internships at *Vogue*.) Americans are competitive, so you would think money would be an easy topic of conversation. But it isn't that simple. It's actually very difficult to talk about something that you believe reflects your worth. America is a society with less of a social safety net than England, where socialism of any kind (socialized medicine, welfare) is practically equated with communism by some, and resented. The trouble with Americans' self-sufficient attitude is that it can engender a lack of sympathy with those living in poverty—an estimated 15 percent—mostly through no fault of their own. So as long as we don't talk about money, we can pretend this inequality is not a problem. The rich want to see themselves as deserving, and the poor don't want to be looked down on for their bad luck. "Equal opportunity" is a nice ideal, but it doesn't really reflect reality in America, or in England, today.

Although England and America each have their own measures of poverty, a slightly higher percentage of people—about 20 percent of the population—falls into the category in England. A Channel 4 documentary, called *Benefits Street*, dealt with the problem of long-term unemployment and welfare dependence on James Turner Street in Birmingham, where up to 90 percent of residents receive benefits. It was controversial—condescending to its subjects, who complained they had been misled about the aim of the program. Others have been more successful at putting a sympathetic face to the problem. In 2011, Jack Monroe, on her blog, "A Girl Called Jack," described her struggle to feed herself and her toddler son on ten pounds per week in a post called "Hunger Hurts": "Poverty isn't just having no heating, or not quite enough food, or unplugging your fridge and turning your hot water off. It's . . . not cool, and it's not something that MPs on a salary of £65k a year plus expenses can understand, let alone our PM who states that we're all in this together. Poverty is the sinking feeling when your small boy finishes his one weetabix and says 'more mummy, bread and jam please mummy' as you're wondering whether to take the TV or the guitar to the pawn shop first, and how to tell him that there is no bread or jam." Monroe has since become a food columnist for *The Guardian* and written a cookbook of budget recipes. Having learned home economy the hard way, Monroe is a welcome voice in a country where recipes in bestselling cookbooks tend to call for a couple of teaspoons each of expensive and exotic ingredients.

Since the recession, Americans and the English have relaxed the money-talk taboo. Saving and economizing have become viable topics of conversation. There are still things they won't talk about: salary, for one. Even among bankers, who talk about other people's money all day long, there is a strong prohibition on discussions of individual salaries. (This is encouraged by managers, who have a vested interest in their employees' ignorance of discrepancies in their pay.) House prices were once considered fair game for discussion, but with the mortgage crisis this has changed. Once, complaining about the size of your mortgage was a stealth brag, since what you could borrow was thought to be indicative of your worth. Not anymore. Money may not be anyone's favorite topic of conversation, but it has taken on a new urgency. People are more likely to speak up about being skint or broke. Maybe because they have realized that they aren't alone, and that it isn't something shameful to hide when many of their friends and colleagues are experiencing the same difficulties. Losing some of their money through little or no fault of their own made a lot of people less likely to think of the poor as lazy or undeserving, and more likely to reexamine their attitudes.

Cuts to England's welfare program have meant that England, like America, is beginning to develop a network of local food banks. People are taking pride in being able to help their neighbors, even though many feel their government has let them down. The welfare state in England is not what it once was. In his annual address to the Lord Mayor's Banquet at London's Guildhall in 2013, Prime Minister David Cameron said that only a smaller state and a "bigger and more prosperous private sector" could prompt an economic recovery.

He called for a "fundamental culture change in our country" to champion "that typically British, entrepreneurial, buccaneering spirit . . . that rewards people with the ambition to make things, sell things and create jobs for others up and down the country . . . We need to do more with less. Not just now, but permanently." He made this speech while wearing a tuxedo and white tie, in front of a room full of similarly clad worthies, who may have been nonplussed by what, at first, sounded suspiciously like an exhortation to go into trade. Luckily, he wasn't talking about them.

Crimbo

In which we explore the pagan side of Christmas with our mutual friend Charles Dickens.

Both Americans and the English complain that the materialistic hype of Christmas begins earlier every year, but Americans don't know the half of it. Without the speed bumps of Halloween and Thanksgiving, England is free to slide straight from the late-summer sales into the roiling commercial bacchanal of Jesus's birthday. Grocery stores begin selling mince pies and Christmas puddings in August. Department stores unveil their seasonal wares in September. Carols may be heard across the land as early as October. So this is Christmas. By December, the English are sick of it, and who can blame them?

"The reason for the season," as pious Americans remind us, has ceased to be the focus in either country. Americans' shorthand for Christmas crosses Him right out: *Xmas*. This has not caught on in England. The English are known for their inventive nicknaming, which makes American attempts at abbreviation appear quaint by comparison. Without some strong context, it would be hard to know what people were talking about half the time. In a country where Paul McCartney is known as "Macca" and Prince Charles as "Chazza," imagine what Jesus is in for. No, don't. The silly nickname the English have invented for Christmas is *Crimbo*. It sounds like an antisocial act that could get you ten to fifteen in a maximum-security gaol (pronounced "jail"—the pokey, the clink, prison). *Crimbo* is more irreverent and less widespread than *Xmas*, but it's also a word more likely to be verbalized, and when it is, it sounds a bit vulgar.

No one calls his grandmother to ask what she's doing for Crimbo, but among friends, at the office, and especially with re-gard to the crasser aspects of Christmas—the shopping, the parties, the drinking, and the romantic opportunism—it's Crimbo all the way. Leigh Francis, star of the popular sketch comedy show *Bo' Selecta!* hit #3 on the charts with "Proper Crimbo," a song about what "Crimbo" is all about: "Put up your Christmas tree (proper Crimbo) / So excited you might wee (proper Crimbo) . . . come sit on my knee / Got gifts for y'all what you got for me?" Ho, ho, ho indeed.

An abbreviation like *Crimbo* serves a strong need that the English have to appear that they don't care all that much. They are far less willing than Americans to declare their intention, unironically, to have a good time, or to put pressure on them-selves to do so. Besides, imagine how you would feel if you were routinely subjected to Christmas carols for the last four months of each year. Enough, already! The urge to "big up" Christmas coexists with the conviction that it is likely to be disappointing in the end, so why not keep expectations low and preserve the possibility of being happily surprised? As a result, many people do report having a better time than they expected, at least, as one friend quipped, if they can remember it the next day.

The Christmas machine is so well oiled that some may be surprised to learn that the traditions of Christmas—and the accompanying anxiety to make it the most wonderful time of the year—are a relatively recent innovation, at least in a country with more than 240 years of history. One man in particular has had a greater influence on the way Christmas is celebrated in England than any other: Charles Dickens. Some have gone so far as to say he *invented* Christmas, though Dickens himself admitted his treatment of the subject had been partly inspired by the American author Washington Irving's lavish depiction of an English country Christmas, published in *The Sketch Book* in 1820, more than twenty years before *A Christmas Carol*.

Dickens's novel enshrined a secular and extravagant ideal that continues to inform most Christmas imagery and advertising today: the family gathered around a feast of turkey and trimmings, the celebration of all that is good and generous, the giving of gifts, and the potentially transformative nature of the holiday itself. If Bob Cratchit can have a proper Crimbo, why can't we? Even Ebenezer Scrooge eventually acquires the holiday spirit, so that "it was always said of him, that he knew how to keep Christmas well, if any man alive possessed the knowledge. May that be truly said of us, and all of us!" (No pressure.) Still, it is worth remembering that *A Christmas Carol*, while remembered for its joyful ending, was billed as a ghost story. The English embrace the dark side of Christmas in a way that Americans do not. They also really know how to laugh it off.

That's why no chapter on Crimbo would be complete without an attempt to explain Panto. That's short for pantomime, which the English essayist Max Beerbohm once described as "an art form specially adapted to English genius." Pantomime has been around, in one form or another, since the Middle Ages. Its current form can be described, pretentiously, as combining the traditions of the British music hall with Italian *commedia dell'arte*. But it's harder to describe in plain terms what Panto is and what it means to the English. Andrzej Lukowski, the theatre editor for *Time Out London*, has said, "Frankly, pantos are so weird . . . I've never managed to explain what they are to somebody who didn't already know."

All pantos share certain conventions. There will be a plot based on a fairy tale or well-known story—*Cinderella*, *Aladdin*, *Peter Pan*, *Puss in Boots*, and *Jack and the Beanstalk* are evergreen. There are archetypal characters, such as the Pantomime Dame, usually played by an older male actor in drag; the Principal Boy, usually played by a young actress in tights; a frothy Fairy Godmother type; and a hammy Villain. The audience will expect big musical numbers, double entendre and innuendo that fly over the heads of children in the audience, slapstick, and, above all, crowd participation. Breaking the fourth wall is standard practice in Panto. Audience members (usually children) will be called up to the stage, often asked to solve a problem or find something or someone who has gone missing. Those left in their seats will help by yelling out, as one, catchphrases like, "HE'S BEHIND YOU!" The actors will shout back, "OH

NO, HE ISN'T," and the audience will respond, "OH YES, HE IS!" It gets extremely raucous, but within certain boundaries that everyone knows and respects. To the uninitiated, Panto can seem like an inside joke on a national scale. It is incredibly silly, but it is also a serious business, lighting up the darkest season of the year.

Eminent actors, writers, and theaters jump at the chance to participate in this seasonal madness. The first Panto I ever saw was at the venerable Old Vic in London. It was a parody of *Cinderella* written by Stephen Fry. In the previous year's production, Sir Ian McKellen had starred as the Pantomime Dame, the Widow Twankey. This allowed the *Guardian*'s reviewer, Michael Billington, to get in on the fun, proclaiming that "at least we can tell our grandchildren that we saw McKellen's Twankey, and it was huge." Pantomime's commercial appeal is ironclad, as it pulls in all ages, both seasoned theatergoers and those who see one play a year. A good one can sell out six to eight weeks' worth of performances in spite of competition from parties and other Christmas entertainments. If you're going to your first Panto, be prepared to laugh yourself hoarse at half the jokes, and to need the other half explained to you.

Pantomime is practically unknown in America. This doesn't mean that American stars can't get in on the action—but it does mean that those who do are usually brought in mainly for their novelty value. In recent years, both David Hasselhoff and Vanilla Ice have played Captain Hook in regional English theaters (Bristol and Chatham, respectively). As I write this, Henry Winkler—*the Fonz himself*—is playing Hook in Liverpool. Emma Samms of *Dynasty* and Pamela Anderson have gamely played a Good Fairy and Aladdin's Genie, though Anderson admitted that when she first agreed to appear in a Liverpool pantomime, she thought it was "miming in a box, which wasn't the case but I already said I would do it." On that note, it seems appropriate to leave Crimbo with the ominous words of Jacob Marley's ghost, reminding us that "no space of regret can make amends for one life's opportunity misused."

Tip

In which a gracious art is defended from its detractors.

n English English, the word *tip* has several meanings. As in American English, it can be a gratuity given for service. But a tip can also be a garbage dump. This dual meaning is appropriate, and rather funny, since most English people regard American tipping habits as a load of old rubbish. One of the most common complaints the English make after visiting America is that everyone who serves them seems to have his hand out for a handout. The BBC's Kevin Connolly captured the prevailing spirit nicely when he griped that "almost every transaction you undertake in America is booby-trapped with social awkwardness." One of the more extremely worded complaints came from Max Wooldridge, travel writer for the *Daily Mail*:

I am constantly amazed that everyone in the US has blindly accepted tipping as a way of life. The transatlantic slave trade was tolerated for many years but that didn't make it right. Different world religions are universally accepted but you are free not to subscribe to them . . . But when it comes to tipping, in the US at least, you are forced to participate whether you agree with it or not. And worse, if you moan about it for even a second you are immediately labeled a tight-wad or a pocket-patter.

One would think, given the invective directed toward American tipping by the English, that England and America had wildly divergent tipping practices. This is not the case. Americans are slightly more generous than the English when it comes to tipping. Americans tend to tip 20 percent, rather than the 10–15 percent that is standard in England. But it's the culture around tipping—who and when and why we tip—that is the source of this seemingly disproportionate angst.

Travel websites and newspaper articles bristle with warnings about the "notoriously fearsome" (the *Telegraph*) tipping culture in America. Stories abound of vacationing Brits being chased out of restaurants by American servers, irate at having been tipped half what they expected. One Englishman told the BBC he had abandoned tipping altogether and was instead leaving his servers preprinted thank-you cards. (If he tried this in New York he would have to be carried out of the restaurant in a body bag.) His approach is not the norm—most vacationing Brits go ahead and follow American tipping protocol, even though many later go online and declare it mad (crazy).

Often their annoyance is focused on the fact that most

tipped workers—particularly restaurant servers—do not earn a living wage in America. In some states, their employers are legally allowed to pay them as little as $2.13 an hour, with the understanding that their tips make up the rest. Many English tourists argue that it is shameful for such a rich country to treat its workers so poorly and that they, the consumers, should not have to bear the burden of America's low minimum wage. Not to mention that cash tipping enables tax evasion on the part of restaurants and workers alike. They do have a point. But most high-minded rants about labor laws eventually give way to more mundane concerns: The English find American-style tipping awkward, and they resent being considered cheap if they don't pony up. This particularly rankles when it comes to bartenders. English bartenders don't expect tips, and are happy to be bought the occasional drink by their regulars, who signal their intentions by saying "and one for yourself" when it's time to pay. No wonder they marvel that bartenders in the United States expect one to two dollars per drink. Why should they pay extra to people fulfilling their basic job requirements?

In England all staff over twenty-one are paid a minimum wage of £6.31 per hour (about $9.50), tipped or not. Since the 1943 Catering Wages Act, service employees have been guaranteed a wage that significantly reduces their dependence on tips. In recent years, most restaurants have even embraced the Continental practice of adding a standard service charge that takes the place of a tip, and printing "service included" on their bills to let customers know. A couple of generations in England have grown up with this model, and that explains why the American system seems ridiculous to them. It's not that they are cheap, it's just that tipping is not as universal—or as important—in England as it is in America. The English aren't used to it, and it makes them nervous. Some sources of information on tipping magnify this anxiety with a nannying tone. The TripAdvisor website shames would-be tippers with lines like "In the UK, the price you pay for a spa treatment is all-inclusive. You are not expected to secrete money somewhere about your person in order to tip your masseur!" In the United States, this is considered something of an art form, as is palming the cash for the coat-check person, such that it is never flashed but covertly passed at the same time your coat is returned. In England there is a little metal tray by the coat check and people who choose to tip ping pound coins into it as loudly as possible so their generosity will not be missed by anyone within five feet.

Americans are alternately proud and defensive of their tipping habits. They are not immune from anxiety about tipping, but they are forced to confront it early and often, and developing tipping skills (the math is just the beginning) is a crucial part of their education. A straightforward psychology underlies American-style tipping. Those who choose to tip generously do so because they know service people work hard for little money, they feel guilty about the unequal relationship of the server and the served (perhaps having worked in service jobs themselves), and they want to be seen as generous. Also, they respond to guilt trips. (A coffee shop where I was once a regular had a sign on its tip jar that read KARMA IS A BOOMERANG.) But above all, Americans like to think of their society as one in which hard work is rewarded, and they like these rewards to be at their discretion. Even if they consistently tip 20 percent regardless of service, as many do, they like the idea that they are choosing, case by case, what to give.

The very few American restaurants that have abolished tipping have made international news, even though some of them simply replaced it with a European-style service charge of around 18 percent. Restaurateurs who have done this report that Americans will often choose to tip anyway, or will argue that their tips would have been more generous than the service charge. They dislike the feeling that they have no influence— whether real or perceived—over the quality of service they get. According to a survey by Zagat, 80 percent of Americans prefer tipping to paying a service fee. One woman, commenting on the *Daily Mail's* travel blog, summed it up:

> I found it uncomfortable to be charged a set service fee in our very nice London hotel/restaurant. Some of the wait staff were superb and efficient, some asleep at the wheel, and I felt there should be a differential in compensation. Not a differ- ence between zero and twenty percent, but perhaps a differ- ence between ten to twelve percent and twenty to twenty five percent . . . When I discussed it with the manager, he said their wait staff pools all the tips—a much more socialist orien- tation than an American staff would prefer. Waiters in the U.S. have a more entrepreneurial spirit. Here it isn't viewed as exploitation of low-income workers, but an opportunity for a worker to generate as much extra as he or she cares to.

Ah, capitalism: the entrepreneurial spirit that animates America! Interestingly, how much we tip has been proven not to have much impact on the quality of service we receive, but it is an article of faith in America that a good tip—and the potential to earn tips—makes for better service. Americans are so well known for this attitude that you may be shocked to hear that not only did they not originate the practice of tipping, they once fought to outlaw it.

Tipping is thought to have begun in seventeenth-century England, where the word *tip* referred to cash given to tavern staff. Some sources claim that the letters *T.I.P.* originally stood for "to insure promptitude," but an explanation so tidy has to be apocryphal. Tipping was an established practice among European aristocrats, and the *OED* definition of *tip* captures the attitude in which tips were given: "A small present of money given to an inferior, esp. to a servant or employee of another for a service rendered or expected." Well-heeled and well-traveled Americans encountered this custom and eagerly imported it to America just after the Civil War. It went over like a lead balloon in a society that had been founded on notions of equality. Soon an antitipping lobby formed. Its central document, William Rufus Scott's *The Itching Palm*, denounced tipping succinctly: "Tipping, and the aristocratic idea it exemplifies, is what we left Europe to escape." Tipping was the "mortal foe" of democracy because "unless a waiter can be a gentleman, democracy is a failure. If any form of service is menial, democracy is a failure." Some states attempted to ban tipping altogether, but these bans proved unenforceable and all were repealed by 1926 as tipping gained a foothold. There were still hopes in some quarters that the controversial custom would not last. Scott went so far as to say that "If tipping is un-American, some day, some how, it will be uprooted like African slavery."

That sounds extreme, but it's interesting to note that in Europe, where higher minimum wages and standardized service charges are the norm, waiting tables is seen as a profession, while Americans still regard it as more of a transitional job.

There is ample evidence that servers can increase their take by doing things like writing thank-yous and smiley faces on checks, kneeling next to tables while taking orders, and touching patrons gently on the shoulder—all of which emphasize their lower status and the extent to which their livelihoods depend on pleasing others. As Chelsea Welch, a former Applebee's waitress, wrote in *The Guardian*, "I've been waiting tables to save up some money so I could finally go to college, so I could get an education that would qualify me for a job that doesn't force me to sell my personality for pocket change." Not all tipped employees take such a dim view of the system. For Americans, the individualism tipping affords for server and served alike—the ability to distinguish oneself through superior service or generosity—has triumphed over any fear that it undermines democracy. In fact, over the past one hundred years, Americans seem to have decided that tipping is democratic after all. Whether they will still think so a hundred years from now, who can say? But in the meantime, the English should stop worrying and learn to love tipping—at least when they are visiting America. After all, they started it.

Tea

In which the drink—and the rituals surrounding it—are
shown to be considerably stronger than they appear.

The British Pavilion did not win the 2013 Venice Biennale, but for sheer crowd-pleasing it was hard to beat. With his exhibition *English Magic,* the artist Jeremy Deller struck a balance between exuberance and provocation. There was a mural of a harrier hawk clasping a Range Rover in his talons, payback for the threat to these endangered birds by toffs on the hunt. There were gut-wrenching drawings by jailed ex-soldiers. There was a film of hundreds of people bouncing on a giant inflatable Stonehenge to the tune of David Bowie's "The Man Who Sold the World," played by the Melodians, a steel drum orchestra. But what really got the polyglot crowds going was the tearoom at the back of the pavilion. Everyone formed an orderly queue, acting positively English as they waited patiently for their turn to tell the "tea lady" strong or weak, with milk or without, sugar or no sugar. It brought to mind the World War II–era slogan "Tea Revives the World." On this occasion it was true, and as I took my steaming cup from the tea lady, I suddenly felt really at home.

The tea that brought the international art crowds together that day—and every day of the Biennale—was the near-caustic-strength blended brew known in England as "builder's tea" because a strong, inexpensive, often sugary drink is what a builder on a break might have (though in a recent survey within the construction industry, 44 percent of builders said they preferred coffee). Typical brands you'd find in any home are PG Tips, Typhoo, and Tetley. (Twinings is also popular, but considered a bit posh.) People who haven't spent much time with the English might think that tea-drinking culture is more refined than it is, possibly marked by persnicketiness about blends, china, and the cult of milk-in-first or milk-in-last. George Orwell played into this stereotype with an article he wrote for the *Evening Standard* in January 1946, "A Nice Cup of Tea," in which he claimed that "the best manner of making it is the subject of violent disputes. When I look through my own recipe for the perfect cup of tea, I find no fewer than eleven outstanding points." I'm sure there are more like him out there, but most people from all walks of life seem happy with the basics. An ad for the tea company Make Mine a Builders declares: "This country wasn't built on camomile."

The first thing an English person does on waking, on returning home, on being greeted with good or bad news, or on receiving a guest, is to turn on the kettle. Every English home and office has an electric kettle capable of boiling water quickly, usually in under a minute. This allows tea-making to be a seamless part of everyday life. According to the United Kingdom Tea Council, 96 percent of tea is consumed in the form of tea bags (an American invention), 98 percent of people take milk, and 45 percent take sugar. Residents of the United Kingdom each consume 2.3 kilos of tea per year to Americans' 0.2 kilos. That adds up to 165 million cups per day and 62 billion cups per year. Most tea is drunk at home, but the consistent quality of what's available, in even the humblest places, points to how important this ritual is. It is ironclad and comforting and near universal in England, but it isn't at all sophisticated unless you count the kettle technology.

Most English people, day in and day out, are drinking tea of a strength that Americans would find a little overwhelming. (Not to mention murder on those expensively whitened teeth.) This explains why 25 percent of all milk consumed in the UK is taken with tea. The English claim that this tea has a negligible amount of caffeine. Don't you believe it. A couple of months after moving to London, convinced I was having panic attacks, I realized it was simply overcaffeination at the hands of generous friends and colleagues. Every cup of tea I was offered, I took—it seemed rude not to—to the tune of five or seven per day. The cumulative effects were heart-pounding, hand-sweating jitters that abated as soon as I learned my limits.

Not that I didn't drink tea in America. Lots of Americans do, and from relatively young ages. But according to the Tea Association of the USA, 85 percent of the tea Americans drink is iced. This chimes with my own experience. I grew up in the southeast drinking only iced tea. (Hot tea was considered strictly medicinal, though in colder states it is more popular.) Here's my family recipe:

Boil a pot of water on the stove. Tie five bags of Lipton's
tea together and drop them into the pot. Leave to steep until
the water turns dark brown, about five minutes. Take the tea
bags out. Upend the five-pound bag of Dixie Crystals (granu-
lated sugar), and pour directly from the bag into the pot, stir-
ring, until no more sugar will dissolve in the warm tea. When
the saturation point is reached, sugar crystals no longer melt
but sink to the bottom in a white layer. Pour the tea, which
should now have the consistency of syrup, over ice.

If you order iced tea in a restaurant south of the Mason-
Dixon Line (which I like to call the Dixie Crystals line), you will
be asked, "Sweet or unsweet?" and to answer the latter marks
you immediately as an auslander, possibly a Yankee. In the
northern and western states, all tea is unsweetened unless otherwise specified (and unless bought in ready-to-drink bottles
and cans, which account for 25 percent of the market, worth
$4.8 billion and growing, as of 2012). So a Southerner will find,
to her horror, that Dixie Crystals do not melt in tea that is already cold, but sink forlornly to the bottom of the glass. For
some Southerners, this is the extent of our science education.

The English don't really drink iced tea because it requires a
large quantity of that foreign substance, ice. Americans like to
complain about the lack of ice in drinks throughout the United
Kingdom, and this is largely warranted. I was once served a gin
and tonic in a fancy Pall Mall club with only two cubes in it. And
even the coldness of the renowned martini at Dukes Bar in Mayfair is achieved by freezing the gin and not adulterating it. On
arrival in America at age two and a half, my daughter was given

a cup of water that contained about one-third liquid and two-thirds ice. She stuck her hand in the cup, pulled out a piece, and said, "What's this?" I am raising a stranger.

You can get an iced tea in Starbucks in England, but it qualifies as something of an eccentricity to order one in a restaurant. That doesn't mean you'll necessarily be denied. My mother unknowingly ordered an off-menu iced tea at one of our favorite restaurants, Le Café Anglais. My seat faced the bar and I watched with amusement and some anxiety as the staff conferred, brewed a pot of their nice, strong tea, pulled out a cocktail shaker, filled it with ice, poured, shook, tasted, winced slightly, and brought the mixture to my mother. She said it tasted fine. I'm sure it was better than anything the English are able to get in America, where even the finest hotels will serve a tea bag on a saucer *next to* a cup of lukewarm water—ensuring it will never brew to the desired strength and eliciting the kind of barely suppressed exasperation usually reserved for careless mistakes by small children.

In America, the "pause that refreshes" has traditionally been Coca-Cola. The average American drinks about four hundred Cokes per year, double the English average. But the hot drink of choice, since the time of the Revolutionary War, has been coffee. The Boston Tea Party—an act of protest in which American colonists destroyed crates of tea owned by the British East India Company in 1773—was the culmination of colonial disenchantment with the motherland. Soon after, Americans fought a bloody battle for their freedom. However much they had once loved tea, it was now seen as the drink of the oppressors. Coffee was the choice of a new generation of patriots, and so it remains. Just ask the Red Cross, whose official policy when assisting at a crisis is to offer disaster victims a calming hot drink before anything else. In America, it's coffee. In England, it's tea.

Is it any wonder that Jeremy Deller decided tea was a necessary component of *English Magic*? Asked if he'd included the tea room to reinforce cultural stereotypes, he demurred: "Well, it's very Chinese to have a cup of tea. It's very Indian to have a cup of tea . . . But that's not an artwork. There's no art there. It's just somewhere to sit, you know?"

Way Out

*In which the Moore family comes to an enchanting place,
and we leave them there.*

To a new arrival or a tourist, English street signs can seem very weird. Sure, there's MIND THE GAP, and they are serious about that one—the "gap" between a Tube carriage and the platform in some stations being wide enough to lose a whole family in, or at least an ill-fitting shoe or carelessly dangled bag. But there is also the HUMPED ZEBRA CROSSING, which sounds like a zoo genetics experiment gone horribly wrong. (Really it's just a pedestrian right-of-way with a *sleeping policeman*—also known as a speed bump—in the middle.)

Some signs might even take on existential significance, depending on the mood in which you first encounter them. Months before our wedding, Tom and I came across a road sign that read CHANGED PRIORITIES AHEAD, and the phrase has been a minor touchstone for us for the past fifteen years (though we never did figure out what it meant in the context of the road work that was taking place in Oxford that day).

As a student, in England for the first time, I was charmed by the signs everywhere reading WAY OUT. This is the English version of the simple EXIT and it spoke to me then of the odd and disconnected way I felt arriving to spend a whole year in a country where I didn't know a soul and no one knew me. England seemed "way out"—so exhilaratingly strange. I could take nothing for granted. After a while, these signs stopped seeming so foreign. But apparently I myself did not. I'm perpetually mistaken for a tourist, constantly asked how long I'm staying or, more to the point, when I'm going "home." There was a time when this seemed like a problem.

For a couple of years after moving to London, I felt we'd made a mistake, trading our life and stable friendships in New York for an uncertain future in a place where we might always be strangers. Before I left America, I never realized how American I was in every word, attitude, and mannerism, or that a common language would not be enough to bridge the gap between American and English culture. For a while, that gap seemed big enough to lose myself in. It wasn't until I left my job in New York and committed to London fully that I began to feel like it could be home. Making friends who embraced our differences and found them fruitful and interesting allowed this fish out of water to breathe again.

These days, I'm always happy to get back to America for a visit, but it's hard to ignore the things about my home country that feel foreign after years away. The frenetic pace of New York is so overstimulating that it keeps me awake all night, wonder-

ing whether I ought to be in the gym, at a bar, or getting a pedicure at midnight just because I can. Leafy London is somnolent
by comparison. The cars, stores, and houses in the suburban en-
claves where our families live feel enormous and unwieldy. A
friend's "modest" suburban house is almost as big as the grocery
store we frequent at home. Even so, the chance to reconnect
with friends and family puts me at ease and, after a few days, I
re-adapt. The transition back to England, by contrast, is usually
seamless now.

When our daughter was born, my husband and I were eager
for her to have the experience of growing up in two cultures at
once. What we didn't understand at the time was that our child
would not feel American at all. She is not experiencing England
as a different culture since it's the only one she's ever known.
She's confused when American friends and family ask how we
feel about living "abroad" and when we think we might come
home. Anne *is* home, with her English passport, her English accent, her school uniform, and her bedroom at the top of a Geor-
gian house.

When Tom and I arrived in England by ourselves, not much
made sense about the move, except our earnest desire to "make
a go of it," as the English say. But when we chose to stay, we chose
as a family, and it made all the sense in the world. More and
more, I realize that home is wherever my husband and children
are—and wherever people love and welcome us. Home is not a
country; home is other people. It has no boundaries and we don't
need a passport or a plane ticket to get there. There is no exit
plan, no way out. We could live anywhere we like, but we like it
here.

Acknowledgments

I am indebted to Lynne Truss and George Lucas, for inspiring and believing in me; Charlie Conrad, for commissioning this project, for his invaluable advice, and for the benefit of his experience; William Shinker, for his friendship and mentorship, and for countless opportunities including this one. Thanks to the team at Gotham Books: Sabrina Bowers, Stephen Brayda, Leslie Hansen, Lisa Johnson, Lauren Marino, Beth Parker, Janet Robbins, Andrea Santoro, Susan Schwartz, and Brian Tart.

I am grateful to many friends for their help and support, including: Benjamin Abel, Catherine Blyth, Dan Bobby, Noel Bramley, Daniela Burnham, Lisa Gladwell Calhoun, Erin Delaney, Kathryne Alfred Del Sesto, Paul Dougherty, Jessica Johnson Downer, Leslie Eckel, Maggie Elliott, Dominique Garcia, Anthony Goff, Ellen Goodman, Amy Grace, Anne and Peter Hatinen, Alex Helfrecht, Steven Hill, Trish Hope, Catherine

Ingman, Rachel Kahan, Sterling and Jon Lanken, Sara Lodge, Bristol Maryott, Doug Miller, Peter Morris, Carole Murray, Ashley Green Myers, Helen Madeo Niblock, Charlotte Nicklas, Elizabeth and Michael Psaltis, Jenna and Arvind Rajpal, Lizzie Reumont, Kathy Richards, Erica Arnesen Roane, Alastair Roberts, Shelagh Rotta, Ann and Peter Rothschild, Fiona Saunders, Michael Sellman, Andrew Shore, Rhian Stephenson, Jörg Tittel, Lucia Watson, Mike Weeks, Crystal Weiss, Hannah Wunsch, and Gina Zimmerman.

Thanks to my parents, Lynne and Alan Bush, for letting me go, and for their unconditional love; to Barbara and Andrew Moore, and their extended Anglo-American family, for always treating me like one of their own; and to Marie-Laure Fleury, whose nurturing and loving presence in our home has allowed me the room to write. My undying devotion to Nana, who will never read this, and to my darlings Anne and Henry, who will. And finally, my love and gratitude to Tom Moore, who makes everything we've ever dreamed of seem possible.

Selected Bibliography

Books

Amberg, Julie S., and Deborah J. Vause. *American English: History, Structure, and Usage*. Cambridge: Cambridge University Press, 2009.

Askwith, Richard. *Feet in the Clouds: The Classic Tale of Fell-Running and Obsession*. London: Aurum Press, (reissue) 2013.

Austen, Jane. *Emma*. New York: Penguin Classics, 2010.

———. *Pride and Prejudice*. New York: Penguin Classics, 2009.

Bailey, Richard W. *Speaking American: A History of English in the United States*. Oxford: Oxford University Press, 2012.

Baron, Dennis E. *Grammar and Good Taste: Reforming the American Language*. New Haven: Yale University Press, 1982.

Bickerton, Anthea. *American English, English American: A Two-Way Glossary of Words in Daily Use on Both Sides of the Atlantic*. Bristol: Abson Books, 1973.

Bolton, W. F., and David Crystal, eds. *The English Language, Volume 1: Essays by English and American Men of Letters 1490–1839*. Cambridge: Cambridge University Press, 1966.

———. *The English Language, Volume 2: Essays by English and American Men of Letters 1490–1839*. Cambridge: Cambridge University Press, 1969.

Bradley, Ian, ed. *The Complete Annotated Gilbert and Sullivan*. Oxford: Oxford University Press, 2006.

Bragg, Melvyn. *The Adventure of English: 500 AD to 2000, The Biography of a Language*. London: Hodder & Stoughton, 2003.

Brown, Penelope, and Stephen C. Levinson. *Politeness: Some Universals in Language Usage*. Cambridge: Cambridge University Press, 1987.

Carey, Gordon Vero. *American into English: A Handbook for Translators*. London: William Heinemann, 1953.

Clark, Alan. *Diaries*. London: Weidenfeld & Nicolson, 1993.

Cooke, Alistair. *Letter from America*. London: Penguin, 2007.

Crystal, David. *The Story of English in 100 Words*. London: Profile Books, 2011.

Deutscher, Guy. *Through the Language Glass: How Words Colour Your World*. London: William Heinemann, 2010.

Dickens, Charles. *A Christmas Carol and Other Christmas Writings*. London: Penguin Classics, 2003.

———. *American Notes*. London: Granville Publishing, 1985. Originally published by Chapman and Hall in the complete works of Dickens, 1892.

Dohan, Mary Helen. *Our Own Words*. Baltimore: Penguin, 1975.

Fellowes, Julian. *Snobs*. London: Phoenix, 2012.

Fiske, Robert Hartwell. *The Dictionary of Disagreeable English: A Curmudgeon's Compendium of Excruciatingly Correct Grammar*. New York: Writer's Digest Books, 2004.

Fox, Kate. *Watching the English: The Hidden Rules of English Behaviour*. London: Hodder & Stoughton, 2004.

Fowler, H. W., and F. G. Fowler. *The King's English*. Oxford: Clarendon Press, 1924.

Gill, A. A. *The Angry Island: Hunting the English*. London: Weidenfeld and Nicolson, 2005.

Gladwell, Malcolm. *David and Goliath: Underdogs, Misfits, and the Art of Battling Giants*. New York: Little, Brown, 2013.

Gorham, Maurice. *The Local*. London: Little Toller Books, 2010.

Haydon, Peter. *The English Pub: A History*. London: Robert Hale, 1994.

Hendrickson, Robert. *Yankee Talk: A Dictionary of New England Expressions*. New York: Facts on File, 1996.

Hitchings, Henry. *The Language Wars: A History of Proper English.* London: John Murray, 2011.

Humphrys, John. *Lost for Words: The Mangling and Manipulating of the English Language.* London: Hodder & Stoughton, 2005.

Hutton, Robert. *Romps, Tots and Boffins: The Strange Language of News.* London: Elliott and Thompson, 2013.

James, Lawrence. *The Middle Class: A History.* London: Little, Brown, 2006.

Krapp, George Philip. *The English Language in America, Volume One.* New York: The Modern Language Association of America, 1925.

Le Faye, Deirdre, ed. *Jane Austen's Letters.* London: Oxford University Press, 2003.

Lyall, Sarah. *A Field Guide to the British.* London: Quercus, 2008.

Mathews, Mitford M. *Americanisms: A Dictionary of Selected Americanisms on Historical Principles.* Chicago, University of Chicago Press, 1966.

McWhorter, John. *Our Magnificent Bastard Tongue: The Untold History of English.* New York: Gotham Books, 2008.

Mencken, H. L. *The American Language: An Inquiry into the Development of English in the United States, the Fourth Edition and the Two Supplements,* abridged, with annotations and new material by Raven I. McDavid, Jr., with the assistance of David W. Maurer. New York: Alfred A. Knopf, 1963.

Metcalf, Allan. *OK: The Improbable Story of America's Greatest Word.* New York: Oxford University Press, 2011.

Michaels, Leonard, and Christopher Ricks, eds. *The State of the Language.* Berkeley: University of California Press, 1980. M. F. K. Fisher's "As the Lingo Languishes," pages 267–76.

Mussey, Barrows, ed. *Yankee Life by Those Who Lived It: The Essence of Old New England Captured from the Writings of the People Who Created It.* New York: Alfred A. Knopf, 1947.

Partridge, Eric, and John W. Clark. *British and American English Since 1900.* London: Andrew Dakers, 1951.

Petrow, Steven, with Sally Chew. *Complete Gay and Lesbian Manners: The Definitive Guide to LGBT Life.* New York: Workman, 2011.

Quinn, Jim. *American Tongue and Cheek: A Populist Guide to Our Language.* New York: Pantheon, 1980.

Scott, William Rufus. *The Itching Palm: A Study of the Habit of Tipping in America.* Philadelphia: The Penn Publishing Company, 1916.

Smith, Jeremy. *Bum Bags and Fanny Packs: A British-American American-British Dictionary*. New York: Carroll & Graff, 2006.

Thody, Philip. *Don't Do It!: A Dictionary of the Forbidden*. London: Athlone Press, 1997.

Trollope, Fanny. *Domestic Manners of the Americans*. London, Penguin, 1997. First published in 1832.

Walmsley, Jane. *Brit-Think, Ameri-Think: A Transatlantic Survival Guide*, second revised edition. New York: Penguin, 2003.

Walpole, Hugh. *Portrait of a Man with Red Hair: A Romantic Macabre*. London: Macmillan, 1925.

Waugh, Auberon. *Will This Do?: The First Fifty Years of Auberon Waugh: An Autobiography*. London: Century, 1991.

Waugh, Evelyn. *The Complete Stories of Evelyn Waugh*. New York: Little, Brown, 1998.

Webster, Noah. *A Collection of Essays and Fugitiv Writings on Moral, Historical, Political and Literary Subjects*. Boston: I. Thomas and E. T. Andrews, 1790.

———. *A Compendious Dictionary of the English Language*. 1806.

———. *An American Dictionary of the English Language*. New Haven: published by the author, 1841.

———. *American Spelling Book*. London: Applewood Books, reprint edition 1999.

Weekley, Ernest. *The English Language, with a Chapter on the History of American English by John W. Clark*. London: A. Deutsch, 1952.

Wild, J. Henry. *Glimpses of the American Language and Civilization*. Bern: A. Francke, 1945.

Young, Toby. *How To Lose Friends and Alienate People*. London: Little, Brown, 2001.

Yule, Henry, and A. C. Burnell. *Hobson-Jobson: The Definitive Glossary of British India, A Selected Edition*. Edited by Kate Teltscher. Oxford: Oxford University Press, 2013.

Blogs

Dixon, Thomas. "The History of Emotions Blog." http://emotionsblog .history.qmul.ac.uk/.

Fogarty, Mignon. "Grammar Girl's Quick and Dirty Tips." http:// www.quickanddirtytips.com/grammar-girl.

Liberman, Mark. "Language Log." http://languagelog.ldc.upenn.edu
   /nll/.
Martin, Gary. "The Phrase Finder." http://www.phrases.org.uk.
Monroe, Jack. "A Girl Called Jack." http://agirlcalledjack.com.
Murphy, Lynne. "Separated by a Common Language." http://separat
   edbyacommonlanguage.blogspot.co.uk.
Wicks, Kevin, ed. BBC America's "Mind the Gap: A Brit's Guide to
   Surviving America." http://www.bbcamerica.com/mind-the-gap.
Yagoda, Ben. "Not One-Off Britishisms." http://britishisms.word
   press.com.

Periodicals

The Daily Mail
The Economist
The Financial Times
The Guardian
HELLO!
National Journal
The New Yorker
The New York Times
Stylist
Vogue

Websites

BBC Archive's first-person accounts of life in WWII: http://www.bbc
   .co.uk/history/ww2peopleswar/stories/92/a1110592.shtml.
BBC Lab UK's Great British Class Survey: https://ssl.bbc.co.uk
   /labuk/experiments/class.
Debrett's: http://www.debretts.com.
Macmillan Dictionary: www.macmillandictionary.com.
Ordnance Survey: www.ordnancesurvey.co.uk.
Oxford English Dictionary: www.oed.com.
Urban Dictionary: www.urbandictionary.com.
World Wide Words: www.worldwidewords.org.